NOT FOR MEN ONLY:

STRENGTH TRAINING
FOR WOMEN

NOT FOR MEN ONLY
STRENGTH TRAINING FOR WOMEN

VOLUME 6

THE WEST POINT SPORTS/FITNESS SERIES

Upon the fields of friendly strife
Are shown the seeds
That, upon other fields, on other days,
Will bear the fruits of victory.

Douglas MacArthur
General of the Army

NOT FOR MEN ONLY:

STRENGTH TRAINING FOR WOMEN

Daniel P. Riley
James A. Peterson, PhD

Leisure Press
P.O. Box 3
West Point, N.Y. 10996

A publication of Leisure Press.
P.O. Box 3, West Point, N.Y. 10996
Copyright © 1979 Leisure Press
All rights reserved. Printed in the U.S.A.

(ISBN 0-918438-19-5)

Text photographs by John Palmgren

Unless otherwise noted, credit for all

photographs should be given to

U.S. Army Photographs

The views of the authors do not purport to reflect the positions of the
United States Military Academy, the Department of the Army, or the
Department of Defense.

CONTENTS

Women have as much to gain from a properly conducted program of physical development as do their male counterparts...and in some cases (particularly athletes) even more.

1

Getting Strong

Women who lift weights will lose their femininity.... Women who lift weights will develop huge, bulging muscles.... Women don't have the biological capacity to be strong.... As the "weaker sex", women shouldn't be concerned with physical fitness.... Women athletes don't need to be strong to excel....

The aforementioned are but a few of the seemingly endless list of superstitions and myths which have been advanced as "evidence" as to why women shouldn't be concerned with their level of muscular fitness. Such reasoning implies that while it's appropriate for you to work on your tummy ...shore up your chest line...for god's sake, however, don't be so audacious as to attempt to develop the musculature of your body.

Quite frankly, nothing could be further from the truth than to suggest that women should not be muscularly fit. Women have as much to gain from a properly conducted program of physical development as do their male counterparts...and in some cases (particularly athletes) even more.

Traditionally, society has dictated that when young men reach the tender age of 12, it's time for them to collectively turn their efforts towards athletics. Such a diligent commitment to the competitive arena will, as the tradition goes, enable every young man to notch a point or two on his ticket to manhood. Likewise, young women, upon reaching 12 years of age, are consciously and subconsciously directed to "get ready for the dating game." Activities which involve rigorous exertion and require higher-than-normal levels of physical fitness (such as competitive sports) are encouraged to be avoided since they will "hinder" the feminity of the participant.

"Total fitness" is no longer considered a male domain. Women of all ages are becoming involved in programs and activities designed to enable them to be "muscularly fit".

Fortunately, the traditional self-concept of women towards developing themselves physically has undergone radical changes in recent years. In many instances, this new-found sensitivity has led to a re-examination of what is "appropriate activity" for women.

One does not have to look too far to see these changes. The sports pages of newspapers are full of the accomplishments of women athletes. Television extols the efforts of women undertaking somewhat Herculean tasks such as the marathon swimming efforts of Diana Nyad, the gymnastic performances of Nadia Comenici, and the marathon running achievements of Kathrine Switzer. Perhaps of greatest import for women of all ages and all levels of fitness is the fact that "total fitness" is no longer considered a *male domain*. Women of all ages are becoming involved with programs and activities designed to enable them to be physically fit. Fortunately, one of the positive by-products of this new-found "physical consciousness" is a trend towards women being interested in increasing their level of muscular fitness (strength and endurance). As a result, women are demanding equal access to the best equipment and to proper training regiments. College weight rooms are no longer restricted to the "football team." Similarly, community "fitness centers" no longer cater exclusively to a male clientele.

Gradually becoming a vanishing breed are the "self-ordained" health clubs which offer women nothing more than a glorified social club, containing only a few machines most of which are similar to the ones which are frequently used in commercials on which the women sit on revolving rollers. Machines such as these and the individuals who literally prey on an unsuspecting public have little or nothing to offer. Psychologically, these machines enable an individual to feel that improvement is occurring simply because of the relatively pleasant sensation produced by their blood rushing to the area of their body being "exercised" in the machine.

In the void created by the vanishing breed of social/health clubs, hundreds of fitness centers have arisen which are designed to serve the fitness needs of their constituency. These fitness centers more often than not include programs specially designed for women, the latest in training equipment, and a sincere desire to offer a sound conditioning program.

Women who are interested in developing themselves physically— tightening up those sagging body parts, eliminating some of their unsightly body fat, attaining a level of muscular fitness which will enable them to do the things they want to do—should undertake a three-step process:

1. Determine how physically fit they are.
2. Identify how physically fit they want to be.
3. Based upon their answers to #1 and #2, develop a program for overcoming the difference between what they are and what they want to be.

Any program designed to achieve all-around (total) fitness must include some form of strength training.

Although not exactly rooted in scientific principles, the first step can be simply accomplished by asking yourself two general questions: Do you look the way you want to look? Are you physically able to do what you need to do either at work or at home. (Note: We strongly believe that *all* women athletes should regularly engage in a strength development program. Chapter 2 discusses the need for strength training by women athletes in greater detail.) If your answer to *both* questions is affirmative, you need take no further action. However, if your answer to either question is "no", then you should proceed to step #2.

Depending upon your own situation (particularly if you're over 30 years old), you may need a doctor's advice to answer the step #2 questions: How physically fit do I reasonably want to be? How physically fit can I reasonably hope to be? If you have the time and resources, there are also a number of excellently-written books which can offer helpful information to the inquiring woman.

In some ways, the third step is the easiest. Develop a program on how best to achieve your personal goals. Any program designed to achieve all-around (total) fitness *must* include some form of strength training. Commit yourself to a program which is both sensible and scientifically sound. The specific overall conditioning program will vary somewhat from individual to individual depending on personal goals, equipment available, etc. At all times, remember, don't try to overcome the abuses of months and years of self-neglect overnight.

The next step is up to you. Start *getting strong* today.

2

The Winning Edge

Without exception, a stronger athlete is a better athlete. While most coaches and athletes generally hold this to be true, far too few take the time and effort to implement this fundamental tenet into their athletic programs. In too many instances, coaches, for one shallow reason or another, fail to incorporate a properly organized strength training program into their overall conditioning program. These coaches claim that they don't have enough time...sufficient equipment...in comparison to other things which need to be done strength training isn't important enough...etc. What these individuals fail to understand is that regardless of the sport, a higher level of strength will benefit *any athlete*. The list of benefits is almost endless — a stronger athlete will be able to run faster, jump higher, throw more forcefully, be less susceptible to injury, be more able to sustain her best level of performance for a longer period of time, etc.

While not every young woman has the genetic potential to be a Billie Jean King, an Ann Myers, or a Kathrine Switzer, every woman athlete owes it to herself to develop her physical abilities to their maximum potential. An integral aspect of the developmental process must be a properly conducted strength training program. A high level of muscular fitness will pay results where it counts — *on the athletic fields and courts.*

Quite frankly, women coaches and athletes have traditionally (even though on a somewhat restricted basis) relied on their male counterparts to obtain information on how to improve their level of strength. Unfortunately, much of the information provided by their male colleagues is based upon

Simply stated and without exception...a stronger athlete is a better athlete.

either unfounded superstitions or intuitive practices. Far too frequently, coaches of men's teams when developing strength training programs for their athletes simply rely on the techniques and programs used by a coach who is perceived to be successful or by a close personal associate. Such a "hand-me-down" source of information may not be the best information available for developing an effective and efficient program.

There are many methods for developing strength, some more effective than others. The best approach is for every coach and woman athlete to commit themselves to a strength development program which is based upon sound, scientifically-proven principles. While differences will sometimes exist between the specific steps taken to implement these principles because of situational differences between schools and colleges, the need to adhere to proper training principles will always remain.

Given the almost complete lack of attention to the physical capabilities of women by the self-proclaimed "scientific community," it is hardly surprising that the number of superstitions and questionable practices attendant to the conditioning of women athletes is lamentably much too high. Fortunately, based upon personal conversations with several coaches of women's teams and upon the attitudes exhibited by the women athletes on the intercollegiate teams both at West Point and Penn State, women athletes do not appear to be inflexibly bound by blind allegiance and adherence to unfounded conditioning practices. As a result, a strong argument can be made in the face of the tremendous, relatively recent, advances in the number of athletic opportunities for women that a sound, legitimate foundation in women's athletics can be established with regard to strength training programs and techniques.

If you're interested in developing to your fullest physical potential, focus your efforts on a properly conducted strength training program. Not only will it enable you to be a better athlete, it will give you *"the winning edge"* to success.

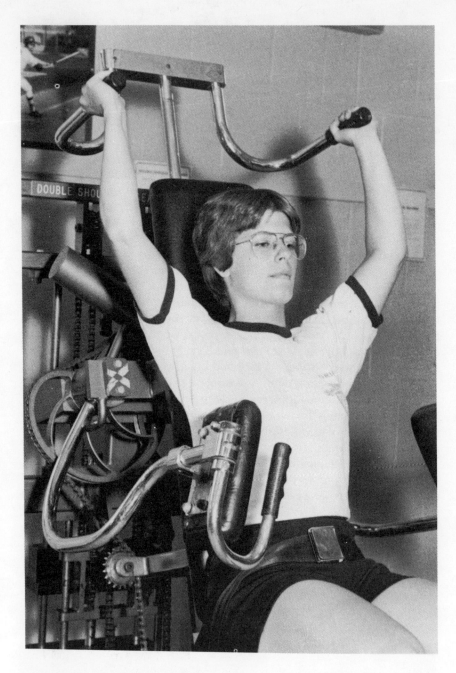

An individual should organize a program which is based on scientific principles, not myths or superstitions.

3

Program Organization

The purpose of this chapter is to discuss how to properly organize a strength training program designed to stimulate maximum gains in muscular strength in the least amount of time.

At present many programs are organized based upon hand-me-down information—information that has been handed down over the years from the weight lifter, to the body builder, to the coach, and eventually to the athlete. The athlete in turn passes on this information to others and the cycle continues. For a woman, given the cultural mores against strength training by women, the existing body of knowledge relating to strength training by women appears to be particularly lacking.

Too often an individual engages in a strength training program which is used by a successful athlete or team. It is assumed that the successful athlete "knows of" the best methods available. In some instances, this may be true; but more often than not, the successful athlete is successful because she happens to be blessed with more "talent" than others, not necessarily because of her methods of conditioning.

An individual need not rely on hand-me-down information to organize her strength training program. An individual should organize a program that is based upon scientific principles, and not on someone's intuition regarding what is the best way to organize a program.

When organizing a strength development program, an individual is primarily confronted with seven variables which should be manipulated. Realize that there are many ways in which these variables can be altered to increase strength. However, we have observed that specific techniques will produce maximum gains in the least amount of time. For the best results, you should not deviate from the information and recommendations presented in this text.

The seven variables of a strength training program include the following:
1. How many repetitions should be executed?
2. How much weight should be used during each exercise?
3. How many sets of each exercise should be performed?
4. How much rest should be taken between exercises?
5. How many workouts per week?
6. In what order should the exercises be performed?
7. What exercises should be performed?

How Many Repetitions?

An individual should perform somewhere between eight and twelve repetitions (reps) of each exercise. Many research studies have observed that significant gains in strength will be obtained when somewhere between six and twelve reps of each exercise are performed.

Most individuals, particularly athletes, are primarily concerned with developing the anaerobic (without oxygen) muscular system. It has been observed that the anaerobic muscular system appears to be most effectively developed when exercised continuously somewhere between 40 and 70 seconds.

We advocate that an individual allow six seconds to execute each repetition. Therefore, perform at least 8 reps (8 x 6 sec. 48 sec.) and not more than twelve reps (12 x 6 sec. 72 sec.), staying within the most effective limits for developing the muscular system.

An individual can obviously increase her level of strength if fewer than six repetitions are performed. However, when only a few reps are performed, the weight must be increased; and this would invite possible injury. Why risk the chance?

When more than 12 repetitions are performed (for the muscles of the upper body), an individual begins to make a gradual transition to the aerobic (with oxygen) muscular system.

Maximum gains will be obtained when somewhere between *eight* and *twelve* repetitions are performed.

How Much Weight?

An individual should initially learn how to properly perform each exercise before progressing to an effective weight. Once the correct techniques have been learned, the individual, through trial and error, should select a weight that will cause her to reach the point of muscular failure somewhere be-

Figure 3-1. If the lifter cannot recover to the starting position, she has reached the point of failure.

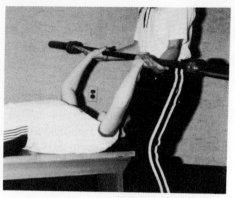

Figure 3-2. If the lifter cannot straighten her arms, she has reached the point of failure.

tween eight and twelve repetitions. The point of muscular failure has been reached when the individual can no longer raise the weight in good form through the muscle's full range of movement. Figures #3-1 and #3-2 illustrate an individual reaching the point of failure on the squat and bench press exercises.

If an individual fails before she reaches eight repetitions, the weight is too heavy. If she can properly perform more than twelve repetitions, the weight is too light and more weight should be added. The "overload principle" must be observed if the athlete is to increase her level of strength. The overload principle simply states that in order for improvement to occur, a demand must be placed on the muscular system. In theory, the demand should be increased each workout session to accommodate the increases in strength. However, an individual should NEVER sacrifice form or technique to do so.

An individual should avoid "all-out attempts" to determine *how much* weight can be lifted. In most instances, this eventually leads to injury and is not as productive as performing more reps with less weight. Remember it is not *"how much"* weight you lift that produces results, but *"how"* you lift the weight.

How Many Sets?

A set involves the number of repetitions executed each time an exercise is performed. One *"properly performed"* set will stimulate maximum gains in muscular strength and endurance. If an individual properly performs one set, she will certainly not feel able to perform a second set; and if she did perform additional exercises, it could eventually become counter-productive. If a second set is performed at a high level of intensity, it is obvious that the first set was not properly performed.

Too many individuals associate gains in strength with the number of sets performed totally disregarding that it is how each exercise is performed that stimulates strength gains. When multiple sets are performed, the individual can be observed "holding back" and pacing herself for the last set to be executed. This method of training can produce significant gains yet the time spent is prolonged and unnecessary.

The objective of an individual should be to organize a workout that will produce the best gains in the least amount of time. The two hour workout is a technique of the past for the individual who properly performs one set of each exercise. A properly performed exercise must include the following five checkpoints:

1. Full range exercise.
2. Allow only the muscles to raise the weight.
3. Emphasize the lowering of the weight.
4. Reach the point of muscular failure between eight and twelve reps.
5. Supervision.

Checkpoint #1. Full Range Exercise

The weight should be raised and lowered (observe Figures #3-3 and #3-4) through the full range of movement. Figure #3-5 illustrates an individual not raising the weight through the full range of movement. Individuals tend to make an exercise easier by not going through the muscle's full range of movement. This allows them to lift "more weight" and *improperly* perform more reps.

The weight should be raised and lowered through the full range of movement to develop strength through the full range and to maintain (and hopefully increase) flexibility.

Checkpoint #2. Allow One-Two Seconds To Raise The Weight

An individual when raising the weight should eliminate all bouncing, jerking, and throwing type movements for two reasons:

1. It places more strain and stress on the muscles, tendons, ligaments, and bones leaving the athlete more susceptible to injury.
2. Some momentum would be used to raise the weight.

Figure #3-6 illustrates an individual attempting to raise the weight using both muscle and momentum. The brain will recruit only as many muscle fibers as are needed to raise the weight. If any momentum is involved, the body will recruit fewer muscle fibers than would have been recruited if no momentum was involved.

Allowing approximately *"one to two seconds"* to raise the weight eliminates the use of momentum in raising the weight and provides for a much safer form of exercise.

18

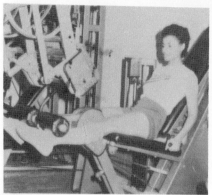

Figure 3-3.

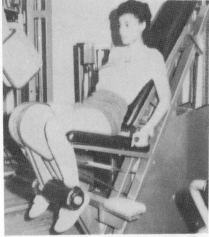

Figure 3-4.

Figure 3-6.

Figure 3-5.

Figure 3-7.

19

Figure 3-8.

Figure 3-9.

Figure 3-10.

Checkpoint #3. Emphasize The Lowering Of The Weight

The lowering of the weight (allow four seconds) is emphasized for the following reasons:

The same muscle that raises the weight is also the muscle used to lower the weight. Therefore, one-half of the exercise is the raising of the weight and the other half is the lowering of the weight. Unfortunately, most individuals are only concerned with "how much weight they can lift," and usually ignore the lowering or "other half" of the exercise. In Figures #3-7 and #3-8, the individual is using the biceps to *raise* the weight and in Figures #3-9 and #3-10 she is *lowering* the weight with the same muscle—the biceps.

An individual can lower a great deal more weight than she can raise. Therefore, in an attempt to maintain the intensity of the exercise, an individual should take twice as long (four seconds) to lower the weight.

Checkpoint #4. Reach The Point Of Muscular Failure Between Eight And Twelve Reps

As previously stated, an individual should continue exercising until she has reached the point of muscular failure. This is the one item of a properly performed exercise that is frequently not followed. Too often an individual stops exercising before the point of muscular failure has been reached. If an individual can properly perform another repetition and she doesn't, she has not gained as much from the exercise as she could have.

Remember, a submaximal effort produces submaximal results. Figure #3-11 illustrates an individual completing a repetition of the leg press exercise. If the individual can fully extend her legs and she stops exercising at

Figure 3-11.   Figure 3-12.

that point (Figure #3-11), she has not reached the point of momentary muscular failure. An individual has reached the point of failure when she can no longer properly complete a repetition as indicated in Figure #3-12. Few individuals train to the point of muscular failure. As a result, few women gain as much strength as they could. This is the most frequently violated checkpoint. Most individuals simply do not push themselves hard enough. The intensity of their exercise is *much too low.*

Checkpoint #5. Supervision

Each repetition of each exercise should be supervised to insure that the proper techniques are being used. It is virtually impossible to train to the point of muscular failure using the techniques previously mentioned when exercising alone or unsupervised.

An adequate amount of supervision can be attained, in most instances, when individuals pair off and train together. Coaches of athletic teams, for example, should *always* insure that their athletes are supervised.

The responsibilities of the training supervisor should include the following:

1. Sound off with a cadence (1001, 1002, 1003, etc.) during the raising and lowering of the weight to insure proper execution.
2. Verbally encourage the lifter to continue exercising to the true point of muscular failure.
3. Should the lifter fail before she properly performs eight repetitions, the spotter can help the lifter raise the weight only as much as is needed to perform a few additional reps (Figure #3-13).
4. If the weight is too light, the spotter can apply additional force on the bar forcing the lifter to fail on or before the twelfth repetition (Figure #3-14).
5. Record on a workout card the amount of weight being used and the number of repetitions performed for each exercise (Figure #3-15).

Figure 3-13.

Figure 3-14.

Figure 3-15. Spotter records weight and reps on the workout card.

How Much Rest Between Exercises?

An individual should move from one exercise to the next while not allowing any time to rest between exercises. If we were to observe a "typical" workout, we would typically find a lifter spending more time resting between exercises than she would spend actually lifting weights.

This method of training leads to a time-consuming, prolonged training session. An individual could obtain the same gains in muscular strength and mass by moving from one exercise to the next in a non-stop fashion. This method of training consumes less time and places a greater demand on the cardiovascular system, thereby increasing the individual's overall level of fitness.

How Many Workouts Per Week?

A muscle must be exercised every 48-72 hours or it will begin to atrophy (grow weaker). Also, a muscle when overloaded, needs at least 48 hours to fully recover. For athletes, during the season, we advocate that an athlete train three times per week while alternating days. During the season, an athlete should train at least once, and preferably twice a week, to maintain and continue to gain strength during the season. (Refer to Chapter 11 for more information on in-season training). For non-athletes, we recommend a year-round training regimen of three times a week on alternate days.

In general, an individual should experience an increase in strength each and every workout. If an increase in strength is not recorded each succeeding workout, the individual:
1. Did nothing the previous workout to stimulate an increase in strength.
2. Performed too much exercise the previous workout.
3. Didn't allow enough time to recover between workouts.

Many individuals, unfortunately, associate progress with the *quantity* of exercise performed. If an individual does not allow at least 48 hours rest between workouts, a point of leveling off will be reached and an eventual regression or loss in strength will be observed clearly indicating that the individual is overtraining.

Order Of Exercise

Whenever possible, the individual should exercise the potentially larger and stronger muscles of the body first. The lifter should progress from the muscles of the legs, to the torso, to the arms, and finish with the muscles of the abdomen.

While exercising the muscles of the torso and the arms, the individual should attempt to alternate pushing and pulling movements whenever possible. Although in most instances any order of exercises could be followed and the individual would get stronger, you should remember that one of your major goals, whenever possible, is to make your conditioning program as efficient as possible. *Do Not Sacrifice Efficiency!*

A great deal of flexibility exists in determining the order of exercise. There isn't any specific prescribed order that appears superior to another. We recommend that the order of exercise be changed periodically to create some variety.

When determining your order of exercises, you should group your exercises by their designated body part (legs, torso, arms, neck) and alternate pushing and pulling movements for the torso and arm muscles.

Legs—buttocks, quadriceps, hamstrings, calves.

Torso—deltoids, lats, pectorals, lower back.

Arms—triceps, biceps, forearms.

Neck—flexors, extensors, trapezius.

Abdomen—obliques, rectus abdominis, transverse abdominis.

Exercises To Be Performed

The exercises to be performed will be dependent upon the equipment available. The exercises performed are not necessarily the key to the program. The key to any exercise program is strict adherence to the aforementioned five checkpoints. You can be assured that maximum gains will be obtained if the methods and techniques mentioned previously are followed. A lifter is forced to utilize the equipment she has available. At least one exercise should be included for each major muscle group in the body. The total number of exercises performed for the muscles of the legs, torso, and arms generally should not exceed thirteen to fourteen. Chapter 9 discusses alternative strength training exercises when specific equipment is not available.

Remember, there are many ways in which a person can increase her level of strength. The methods mentioned herein are designed to produce *maximum gains* in the *least amount of time.*

Refer to Chapters 6, 7, and 8 for prescribed exercises using barbells, Universal Gym, and Nautilus equipment.

4

Methods And Techniques

To many individuals, strength training has been accepted as a valuable tool for preventing injury and improving performance. Unfortunately, only a few athletes and coaches take the time to develop an in-depth understanding of the most recent changes in the body of knowledge relating to strength training.

Regrettably, most coaches continue to use those methods and techniques that they have been using over the years. They pass these methods along to their athletes, and the cycle of using the same techniques is continued. A few coaches simply rely on what other coaches are doing. The programs of individuals and teams perceived to be successful are emulated merely because of the hope that adherence to these programs will result in similar success.

We strongly recommend that coaches base their strength training programs on scientific principles. Strength training programs should always be based upon sound, scientifically-proven information, not merely on what someone else is doing (even if another team happens to be successful). This is one of the major reasons why many coaches change their programs every year. They want to be doing what the winner is doing. More often than not, however, teams are successful simply because they have great athletes. Strength training programs should always be based on the best information available so that maximum gains can be assured.

Testing Strength

The *only* concern for testing strength should be to evaluate the progress of each lifter. The purpose should be to insure each individual is indeed getting stronger.

At Penn State, for example, the athletes are tested each workout. The Penn State athletes are required to record the amount of weight used and the number of reps performed each time an exercise is done. As a result, a coach can look at any athlete's workout card and observe the progress from workout to workout. If progress has not been made from workout to workout, something may be wrong.

We recommend that coaches use the same methods to test their athletes as they do to train them. Coaches can more effectively evaluate the increases in strength (however slight) from one training session to the next by using the same methods to both test and train. Since skill is not involved when the same techniques are used to both train and test an individual, the risk of injury that occurs occasionally when max reps are performed is virtually eliminated.

When different methods are used to train and test athletes, certain difficulties are encountered. For example, probably the most commonly used method for measuring "strength" is to test athletes on how much weight they can lift one time (max rep) on a few selected exercises. A major problem that arises with this testing protocol is that a max rep is simply not a very reliable measurement. For example, on the athlete's first attempt she bench presses 150 pounds. She feels she can lift more weight, so on her second attempt she tries to lift 165 pounds and fails.

Does this mean that her strength level is 150? Not necessarily so. If the individual attempted 165 on her first attempt (not having fatigued the muscles with a previous heavy lift) possibly she could have made the lift at 165, or 160, or 170, or who knows what. In addition, a coach might identify the exact weight that an athlete could lift on Monday to be 170 pounds, while on Friday the same athlete cannot lift the same 170 pounds.

The bottom line on testing is that any all out attempt—be it a bench press, a mile run, or a high jump—is very unreliable. World class high jumpers seldom jump the same height in two successive meets. Runners seldom run as fast or even near their best time in successive meets.

Two of the world's noted exercise physiologists, Astrand and Rodahl, state that "Muscle strength is a very complicated function and the number of muscle fibers available is only part of the story. It is not surprising that even in well-standardized measurements of muscle strength, the standard deviation of the results obtained in repeated tests on the same subject is of the order of ± 10 percent or even higher. The practical application of measurements of muscle strength is therefore doubtful."

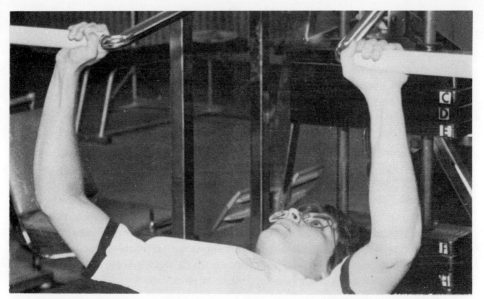

Testing max reps for any exercise does not accurately predict an individual's ability to play a sport.

With some justification, coaches feel that testing an athlete's level of strength serves as a great motivating factor. If you must test, use the same methods to test that you use to train. An athlete can more easily reproduce an effort of somewhere between 8 and 12 repetitions workout after workout.

Testing by using one max rep will eventually encourage a lifter to train using those testing principles knowing that she will be tested on only the one max rep. Training methods used to perform the one max rep are not as productive as the methods discussed in Chapter 3. In addition, the techniques employed for max reps consume a great deal more time and are far more dangerous to the safety of the individual.

Testing max reps for any exercise does not predict the player's ability to play a sport. For example, many coaches have traditionally believed that the bench press, squat, power clean, etc., were an excellent prediction of strength, athletic ability, etc. There are many individuals, for example, who can bench press a great deal of weight yet are not very good athletes.

An individual with short arms has the potential for bench pressing more weight than an individual with longer arms. Some individuals have certain mechanical and physiological advantages which give them the ability to lift more weight than other individuals. Yet it doesn't necessarily mean that they have the potential to be better athletes than other individuals who "appear" to be not as strong.

Unfortunately, testing max reps may discourage those individuals who are not blessed with the characteristics needed to demonstrate (e.g., bench press a lot of weight) strength. We have seen many outstanding athletes who have been "turned off" to strength training because they felt embarrassed in the weight room because they could not lift enough weight to get into the infamous "300" pound club. Yet on the field the athlete excelled and had the ability and natural strength to physically handle some of those members of the illustrious 300 pound club. As a result, the athlete who is "turned off" never has the opportunity to accrue the benefits of a muscular development program.

Comparisons Between Athletes

Coaches should not make strength comparisons between athletes. There are too many variables that allow some athletes to lift more weight than others. The goals should be to take each athlete from their existing strength level and make each athlete stronger, comparing each athlete only to herself. Compare her gains from month to month or week to week or workout to workout, but don't compare her results to anyone else's.

Testing Athletes

If a coach feels she must test her athletes, we recommend two exercises (for the upper body)—chinups and dips. Chins and dips are used because they are easy to perform (little skill), easy to administer (only chin and dip bars are needed), and relatively very safe (the risk of injury is less than for the exercises traditionally used for "testing" strength, e.g., squat, power clean, etc.).

If the athlete knows she is going to be tested on chins and dips she will probably practice them. The chinup and dip exercises are two of the most productive exercises that can be performed. Athletes should be tested in the same manner that they perform the exercise during a workout. Don't use kicking or jerking movements to raise the weight and take four seconds to lower the body.

The same individuals that are motivated by lifting heavy weights will eventually be motivated by any program that the coach requests. Therefore, use those techniques designed to develop maximum gains in the least amount of time. The max rep (pyramidding) technique may make an individual stronger but at the expense of risking injury, will consume a greater amount of time, and will not produce the intensity of exercise needed to best prepare an individual to be a better athlete.

Speed Of Exercise Vs. Speed Of Movement

At present a controversy exists concerning the relationship between the speed an exercise is performed (how fast should the weight be raised) and its

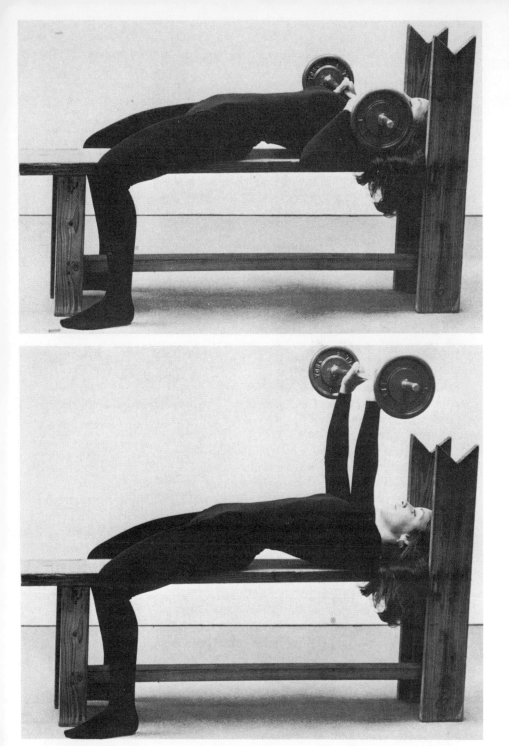

The practice of fast or explosive lifts will build little or nothing in the way of actual strength in the muscles...instead, the individual will learn the skill required to throw the weight...since she certainly isn't lifting it.

Figure 4-2.

Figure 4-1.

affect on the athlete's speed of movement. The primary goal of any strength training program should be to improve an athlete's ability to perform (e.g., run faster, jump higher, etc.).

To improve the athlete's ability to perform a specific physical task, an individual should analyze what the skill involves. Each task should be broken down to analyze the physical aspects attendant to the skill. Once the basic attributes have been identified, a developmental conditioning program can be prescribed to improve each aspect. Consequently, improving each of the attendant attributes, the individual will be a better athletic performer.

When an individual is observed performing an explosive task (e.g., vertical jump) (Figure #4-1), two basic attributes can be identified which allow her to explode from the floor. The first and probably the most important attribute is the individual's neuromuscular efficiency. The second attribute is the strength of the muscles used to perform the skill.

Neuromuscular efficiency is the term used to describe the ability of the brain to transmit impulses through the central nervous system to the muscle fibers being recruited to perform the skill. For an individual to explosively jump from the floor, she just be capable of recruiting a large percentage of her muscle fibers, as quickly as possible, in the proper sequence. The sequence of muscle fibers being recruited is important for a skill to be precisioned. Practice will improve the level of precision. Some individuals have the potential to be more neuromuscularly efficient than others. Remember that every individual's potential is different.

How To Improve An Athlete's Level Of Neuromuscular Efficiency

How, the question may be asked, can a coach improve an athlete's level of neuromuscular efficiency which is used to explode from the floor? The answer is "to have the athlete practice exploding from her stance." Nothing can replace the practicing of a skill to improve that specific skill.

With practice, the individual will develop a refined and specific neuromuscular pattern (specifically of exercise) used to explode from the floor. When the time comes for the athlete to jump explosively, the brain will transmit the same neuromuscular signal each time. Once the skill has been practiced, the same muscle fibers will be recruited at the same speed in the same sequence (excluding fatigue). Simply stated, an individual, through the practice of a skill, can program her brain and muscles to respond in a specific, similar manner every time she attempts to jump from the floor.

Therefore, it is our opinion that the best way an athlete can improve her ability to jump explosively is to practice jumping explosively. To run fast, practice running fast. To throw a softball, practice throwing a softball.

Traditionally, many coaches have believed that by performing power cleans, or squats, or leg presses in an "explosive" fashion the athlete's ability to jump explosively would be improved.

It is now obvious, however, that an individual uses a specific neuromuscular pattern to jump. On the contrary, an athlete will develop and use a *completely different* neuromuscular pattern to perform power cleans, leg presses, dead lifts, squats, etc. Therefore, it appears that there is *no* positive skill transfer in skills performed in the weight room to those performed on the field.

Drowatyky (a noted motor learning expert) states that "presently no evidence exists to support the overload principle (using additional weight for practice) when applied to motor skill learning (p. 22). No support was found for the practice of using added weight during practice to improve performance in motor skills learning (p. 126)."*

A basic guideline should be: Do not perform a skill or exercise in the weight room to imitate or improve a skill on the field. However, do practice and perform the specific skill on the field to improve that specific skill.

Increase The Strength Of The Muscles Used To Perform A Skill

It was stated previously that there are primarily two attributes which allow an individual to jump; her level of neuromuscular efficiency and the strength of the muscles used to perform the skill.

If an individual wants to jump higher (demonstrate explosive power), she should practice jumping (Figure #4-2) in order to perfect the skill (neuromuscular efficiency). Eventually, however, she will reach a point where she virtually levels off and does not jump any higher. The only other means she can

Figure 4-3.

use to increase her vertical jump is to strengthen the muscles used to jump (Figure #4-3). The additional strength will then allow her to jump higher as she continues to practice the skill. Therefore, for any strength training program, an individual should identify and implement those techniques that are designed to stimulate *maximum* gains in STRENGTH. Only by strictly adhering to a properly designed strength development program and practicing the skill can an individual achieve the highest possible level of improvement.

At What Speed Should An Exercise Be Performed?

At what speed should an exercise be performed (how fast should the weight be raised) to stimulate maximum gains in strength? Unfortunately, at present we simply don't know (nor does anyone else) what the "ideal" speed of exercise should be for any athlete. Some coaches feel that athletes should perform strength training exercises at the same speed they perform specific athletic skills. In theory this sounds practical. Yet, when the many different athletes' movements and the speed at which they are performed are observed, it is readily apparent that this is both unrealistic and virtually impossible.

The goal of any individual when lifting a weight should be to increase her level of strength. A basic guideline which should always be followed is to raise the weight as fast as the athlete can, allowing the muscles to do all the work, *without the use of any momentum.* Unfortunately, when an individual hears **fast,** she typically thinks of throwing the weight. This is not recommended. A rule of thumb is to take from one to two seconds to raise the weight. This rule can be strictly enforced by having someone sound off with a verbal cadence (periodically using a stopwatch to check speed).

If an individual can "throw or explode" with a weight, the weight is obviously too light. If a weight was sufficiently heavy, the lifter couldn't throw it even if she wanted to throw it.

Observe Figure #4-4. The individual has performed an explosive pushup with her own bodyweight. It can be observed that although her arms are locked, her body continues upward. She is capable of throwing the body upward because at that point in the exercise her bodyweight is too light and she is capable of throwing it upward. There is a great deal of momentum involved with this form of exercise which prevents the muscles from doing all of the work and gaining as much strength as they should. Yet in Figure #4-5, the same individual attempted to explode or throw her body upward, yet she couldn't. In this instance the additional weight prevents her from throwing or using momentum to raise the weight. The muscles are forced to do all the work precluding the use of any momentum. Again if a weight is heavy enough the individual cannot explode or throw it. Therefore, while raising a weight, an individual should allow her muscles to do all the work if she is to gain as much strength from the exercise as she possibly can.

The brain will only recruit those muscle fibers that are needed to raise a weight. For example, assume that an athlete must recruit 100 muscle fibers to raise 100 pounds. Additional fibers are not needed and will not be used. If fewer than 100 fibers are recruited (when the muscle does all of the work), the athlete would not be able to raise the 100 pounds. Since the brain will only recruit those muscle fibers needed to raise the weight, the lifter should raise the weight at a speed in which the muscle does *all of the work*. If the

Figure 4-4.

Figure 4-5.

Figure 4-6. **Figure 4-7.**

weight is raised too fast, the individual uses some momentum. As a result, fewer muscle fibers will be needed to raise weight. If fewer muscle fibers are recruited, the increase in strength will also be less than it could be.

Figure #4-6 (push-ups) illustrates that it is possible to throw or explode and raise the weight so fast that the muscle at some points is doing little or no work. The weight is actually free falling upward. The brain will recruit fewer fibers during those points where momentum is incorporated. Obviously, such a technique is less productive for gaining strength. An individual should always remember that gaining strength is her primary objective from a muscular fitness program.

While performing any isotonic exercise (barbell, Universal Gym, Nautilus, bodyweight), we recommend that an individual select a weight in which she reaches muscular fitness somewhere around the tenth repetition. During the first few reps of the exercise (approximately 4-6 reps), the weight is actually too light to increase strength. The purpose of these preparatory reps is to gradually recruit more muscle fibers each succeeding rep.

A lifter should actually hold back and control the weight on the first few reps. If an exercise is properly performed and the correct amount of weight is used, an individual could attempt to explode with the weight on the last rep or two but couldn't because at that point, the weight would be so heavy that she couldn't throw it (Figure #4-7).

We have seen every method of strength training that is currently practiced (and then some). Training explosively (throwing and jerking weights in the weight room) is frankly less productive and, unfortunately, extremely dangerous to both the joints and the connective tissue of a lifter.

Power Cleans

A power clean (Figures #4-8 & #4-9) is an exercise that has long been given credit for developing and improving many of the physical attributes requisite of the successful athlete (power, explosive power, speed of movement, etc.). Coaches have been led to believe that the power clean will develop the specific explosive patterns needed by an athlete and that the power clean is one of the most productive exercises that can be performed.

Most of the beliefs associated with the power clean are simply untrue. They are based upon supposition, not facts. The fact is that the power clean is one of the most dangerous exercises that any individual can perform. Why then do individuals perform this exercise? Why do so many coaches continue to subject their athletes to an exercise that is so potentially hazardous to the athlete's well being?

The reasons put forth by coaches and individuals for performing the power clean include:

1. It develops explosive power.
2. It resembles a vertical jump.
3. It involves many major muscle groups making it a good full-range exercise for general overall development.
4. A coach of a successful team said it was a good exercise.

Figure 4-8.   Figure 4-9.

The relationship between the speed of exercise and the speed of movement on the athletic field has already been discussed. A power clean is a specific skill in itself. It has no practical transfer to an individual who is jumping. Throwing and jerking weights up in the air and jumping under them is certainly neither a correct nor even a logical approach for improving a specific skill.

Individuals cannot imitate or duplicate in the weight room a skill performed on the athletic field. Two completely different neuromuscular patterns are used to come and perform the power clean.

When a simple mechanical analysis is performed, jump (for example), it can be seen that the power clean does not take any one muscle through its full range of movement. Muscles are used to get the bar moving off the floor with a sudden pull or jerk. Eventually the bar is being raised upward primarily with momentum (as it must so that the lifter can change direction and jump under the bar).

As previously stated, the proper approach to selecting exercises should be: identify the muscles used to play a sport and prescribe a specific exercise for each major muscle group. Select the best exercise to isolate and develop the lower back, the quadriceps, etc. The power clean does not properly develop or exercise any muscle group through its full range of movement. If the mechanics of the power clean were clearly understood by athletes and coaches, the power clean would not be included in the strength training program.

Negative Exercise

Many individuals hear the term negative exercise and immediately associate it with something "bad." One half of an exercise is the raising of the weight (positive work). The other half of an exercise is the lowering of the weight (negative work). The term negative work simply describes the eccentric part of any contraction. The concentric portion of a muscle contracting is the raising of the weight. The eccentric portion of the exercise is the lowering of the weight.

While performing any conventional isotonic exercise (bodyweight, barbell, Universal Gym, Nautilus), it is impossible not to perform negative work unless someone else lowers the weight for you. The lowering of the weight should be emphasized because it is one half of the exercise. The same muscles which are used to raise the weight are the *same* muscles used to lower the weight. An individual can lower a great deal more weight than she can raise. Therefore, in an attempt to maintain the intensity of the exercise she should take longer to lower the weight (or add more weight during the lowering portion of the movement). Durng conventional exercise (bench press, chinup, dip, etc.), she should take four seconds to lower the weight.

Negative-Only Exercise

Individuals should also take advantage of the benefits of negative-only exercise. The individual only lowers the weight during an exercise performed in a negative-only manner.

Negative-only exercising has many advantages. The greatest advantage can be observed when an individual fails and can no longer raise the weight. For example, while performing pullups, an individual fails on the 4th rep of the exercise. She cannot raise her bodyweight properly to perform a 5th rep. Most individuals will stop performing the exercise at this point. The intensity of exercise after four reps is very low. Additional improvement could be achieved if the individual could somehow continue the exercise for a few more reps. The individual's bodyweight at that point in the exercise is too much to continue any more normal exercise. The individual should then continue to perform the exercise in a negative-only manner. She should somehow get her chin over the bar (Figures #4-10 to #4-13) (step up on a stool or ladder) and just lower her body. While performing negative-only exercise, 8 seconds should be taken to lower the weight.

The same concept can be used with a barbell or any conventional equipment. The spotter can help the lifter raise the weight and let the lifter lower it by herself. The total number of reps to include those performed by the lifter in a normal fashion and those performed in a negative-only fashion should not exceed 12 reps. The spotter should only record those reps on the workout card that the lifter performed in normal fashion.

In the opinion of many exercise physiologists, the use of negative-only exercise is one of the most significant developments in the history of conditioning techniques. Negative-only exercise has particular applications for women. Since many women have a relatively low level of muscular fitness (particularly upperbody strength) due to the cultural inhibitions towards women and "strength", women need to develop a *base level* of muscular fitness. Negative-only training provides a relatively quick, highly effective method for developing such a base. In addition, in many instances, no equipment is required.

At West Point, negative-only training has been the single *most effective* method of developing strength in the entering women cadets. Once a base level of fitness has been established, the women cadets then train on the available conventional equipment (Nautilus, free weights, etc.). Figures #4-10 to #4-16 illustrate two functional negative-only calesthenic exercises.

Negative exercise is a valuable and productive part of an exercise. Do not fear or neglect it. It is just as important as positive work (if not more important).

Figure 4-10. Climb up to the bar.

Figure 4-11. Mount the bar in a flexed-arm hang position.

Figure 4-12. Lower yourself down at a slow, steady pace taking eight seconds.

Figure 4-13. The completion position for a negative-only pullup is the dead-arm-hang position. To perform another rep, repeat steps #4-10 to #4-12.

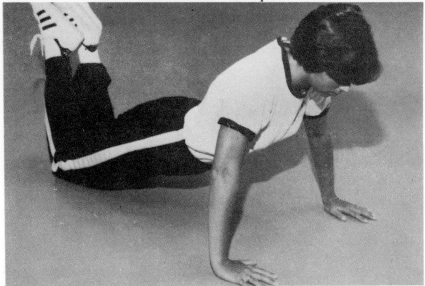

Figure 4-14. Assume a knees-on-the-ground position.

Figure 4-15. Assume a front-leaning-rest position.

Figure 4-16. Lower yourself down at a slow steady pace taking eight seconds.

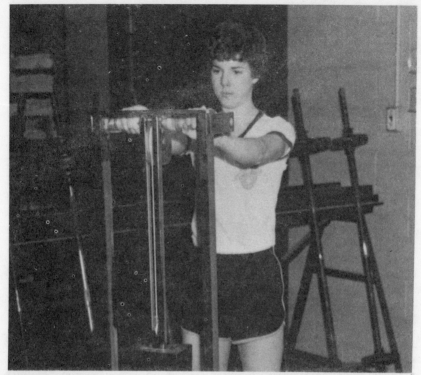

Coaches and athletes should remember that it is not necessarily the tool that you use (that is the key to strength gains), but how you use it.

Negative-Accentuated Exercise

Negative-accentuated training is a method of exercising whereby a lifter uses two limbs to perform the positive portion of the exercise and alternating limbs, uses one limb to perform the negative portion of the exercise. For example, an individual uses both of her legs during the positive portion of the leg extension and lowers the weight back to the starting position using only one leg (Figures #4-16 and #4-17).

The primary advantage of negative-accentuated exercise is the great amount of resistance which can be applied to a single limb (leg or arm) during the eccentric portion of the exercise. The major disadvantages are: specific equipment is required (e.g., Nautilus, Universal, etc.), and negative-accentuated training is restricted to those exercises which involve the lifter's limbs.

Motor Learning Principles and Practices by John N. Drowatyky, Burgess Publishing Company, Minneapolis, MN, 1975.

5

Administering The Strength Training Program

Coaches are frequently faced with the dilemma of organizing and administering a strength training program for a large number of athletes. Unfortunately, the facility usually available is more suitable for handling smaller numbers. Therefore, the coach should utilize those methods of administering a strength training program that are designed to best accommodate a large group of athletes. Careful attention should be given to the selection and organization of the training methods so that the effectiveness of the program is not decreased in any way. The methods presented in this chapter are the most effective methods available to train the largest number of athletes without sacrificing strength gains.

While it may be possible to train more athletes using other administrative procedures, results that could have been obtained will be sacrificed. Realistically speaking, there may be times when the coach is forced to use less productive procedures. We recommend that she adhere as closely as possible to the steps outlined in this chapter.

The typical procedures used when administering the strength program can be observed when the coach unlocks the weight room door and "herds" a large number of athletes into the facility. The athletes are then requested to simultaneously "attempt" to complete a workout. The athlete in this situation is forced to compete with other athletes to obtain and eventually make use of an exercise station.

The "mass entrance into the facility" approach leads to a less productive, chaotic, and haphazard approach to training. Athletes can be observed wasting most of the workout period waiting for an exercise station to become vacant (Figure #5-1). Little time is actually spent lifting. Upon completion of the time allotted, only a few athletes will have performed all of the exercises initially prescribed for the workout. As a result, some of the major muscle groups will have been ignored. In many instances, it is those ignored muscle groups that may be most critical in the prevention of injury.

In order to have a properly conducted strength training program all athletes should employ the same training techniques. Those techniques discussed in Chapter 4 should be utilized. The coach should dictate that all athletes adhere to these techniques. Continuity of the program will be disrupted and maximum gains will not be obtained if these techniques are not strictly enforced by the coach and adhered to by the athletes.

The administrative principles and guidelines outlined in this chapter are fundamental precepts for achieving the most effective and efficient program possible. Admittedly, some situations unfortunately dictate that the coach "herd" a large number of athletes into a facility at one time. If this method of training is her only alternative, by all means she should continue the program as best she can. However, she should make every attempt to incorporate the proper guidelines whenever possible. Adherence to these procedures will maximize the benefits both to the coach and to the athlete.

Initially, to facilitate the supervision of the program, the coach should select a block of time during the day that is most convenient for those athletes participating in the program. If possible, a coach, trainer, or instructor should be present at all times to provide encouragement and the *supervision* needed to coordinate the program.

Figure 5-1.

Proper Administration

The administrative principles of the program would include the following guidelines:

    I. Select a *prescribed order* of exercise with whatever equipment is available.

    II. Assign *training partners* (training teams).

    III. Assign *training times* to each training team.

I. Select A Prescribed Order Of Exercise

The coach should select a group of exercises (using the equipment he has available) designed to develop each of the major muscle groups in the body.

Once the exercises are selected the coach should place them in an order utilizing the guidelines discussed in Chapter 4. Refer to Chapters 6, 7, 8, for specific workouts using the barbell, Universal Gym, and Nautilus equipment.

Once the order of exercise is established it is imperative that all players progress to each succeeding exercise in the exact order prescribed.

Any deviation from the pre-designated order of exercise will disrupt the continuous flow of athletes that should be an integral characteristic of the program.

By including exercises for each of the major muscle groups the coach can be assured that all athletes will develop general overall strength. By demanding that all athletes perform each of the exercises, the coach need not worry that some athletes may be ignoring any one muscle group.

An established order of exercise allows a smooth, consistent and controlled flow of athletes through the exercises. The coach can then calculate approximately how many athletes can be scheduled to work out in the allotted time available.

If the proper time interval is scheduled between athletes starting at the first exercise station, the athlete should be able to move immediately from station to station allowing her to train in a non-stop fashion.

This method of administering the program will produce maximum gains in strength, take less time for the athletes to complete a workout, and allow the coach to train the largest number of athletes within the available time.

Whenever possible, the coach should make every attempt to prescribe only 1 exercise at each station. This provides for a continuous flow of movement by preventing delays at the same station where two different exercises are performed (example: Lat pulldown and triceps extension) (Figures #5-2 & #5-3).

43

Figure 5-2.   Figure 5-3.   Figure 5-4.

II. Assign Training Partners

Training partners should be assigned to supervise the entire workout (Figure #5-4). Maximum strength gains *will not* be obtained unless each repetition of every exercise is performed properly. Supervised exercise is overwhelmingly far more productive than unsupervised exercise.

It is impossible for a coach or a coaching staff to provide one-on-one supervision for each athlete every workout. Supervised exercise can easily be obtained by assigning each athlete with a training partner (who is a fellow teammate). Each will supervise the other through the complete workout. Refer to Chapter 3 for more information about the responsibilities of the training supervisor.

Training partners should have a schedule that is compatible. They need to meet in the facility to train each other at a time that is accommodating to both.

They should have the type of relationship in which they will be capable of "pushing" each other to their full physical and psychological capabilities. Assigning a senior and a freshman to the same training team could create a situation where the freshman may feel inhibited and as a result will not demand an all out effort from her senior counterpart.

Each partner in the "training team" is responsible to the other for always supervising each repetition of every exercise and demanding proper execution. *Never* should an athlete train alone. If a training partner is not able to attend a workout, provisions should be made to obtain a substitute supervisor for that workout.

Figure 5-6. Warm-up before
the workout.

III. Assign Training Times

The coach should prevent a large number of athletes (training teams) from reporting to the facility at the same time. This only causes some athletes to wait an extended period of time before they begin their workouts.

Time delays can be prevented by assigning each athlete a *start time*. A start time indicates the exact time the athlete will be situated at the first exercise station and ready to begin exercising.

A time chart is needed to record each athlete's assigned starting time. Training partners should select a block of time that they can report to the facility, exercise, shower, etc.

A time chart similar to the one illustrated in Figure #5-5 can be used to record names and starting times. We recommend that you cover your chart with acetate so that you can record names, erase them, and reuse the chart.

The lifter and her training partner should report to the facility at least 5-10 minutes before their assigned start time. This time should be used to warm-up and stretch (Figure #5-6) and prepare the workout card (Figure #5-7) by filling in the amount of weight to be used for each exercise. Prerecording the weights on the card will save time once the workout begins.

Once the lifter begins the workout she should continue exercising moving from one exercise to the next in a non-stop manner. The lifter's training partner should escort the lifter from exercise to exercise assuming the responsibilities of a spotter. The lifter should progress to each exercise in the exact order prescribed by the coach.

Upon completion of the workout, the lifter should then return to the first exercise station and supervise her training partner through the same workout from start to finish. The coach can arrange the start times in such a manner that the lifter just completing the workout has a brief recovery period before she supervises her partner through the same workout.

45

Figure #5-5. Scheduling Time Chart*

Time	Lifter's Name	Supervisor
*3:00	*Hamel	*Walter
3:02	Miles	Hall
3:04		
3:06		
3:08		
3:10		
3:12		
3:14		
3:16		
3:18	Barkalow	Utchel
3:20		
3:22		
3:24		
3:26		
3:28		
3:30		
3:32		
3:34		
*3:36	*Walter	Hamel
3:38		

*This time chart indicates that a two minute time interval is scheduled between training teams. Each team consists of two individuals: a lifter and a spotter to supervise the lifter. Hamel, for example, is assigned a starting time of 3:00. Walter is Hamel's spotter. Walter will supervise Hamel's workout from start to finish. Let us assume that Hamel will finish her workout at 3:30. We allow her a few minutes to recover and then assign Walter a start time of 3:36. Hamel will now supervise Walter through her workout from start to finish. Both will be in and out of the weight room, having completed a total body workout, in less than 1 hour.

If the lifter completes her workout at 3:30, the coach can assign the lifter's training partner a starting time of 3:36, allowing the lifter 5 minutes to rest before she becomes a supervisor.

The starting times should be arranged in such a manner that a sufficient amount of time is allowed between each athlete starting the program at the first exercise station. A minimum amount of time should be allowed between athletes to prevent backups at any station. The athlete should be capable of moving from one station to the next without ever having to wait for a station to become available.

Figure #5-7. Prerecorded weights on workout card.					
Name					
Date					
EXERCISE					
Leg Press	220/9	220/11	*225/		
Leg extension	95/11	100/8	*100/		
Leg Curl	80/8	80/9	*80/		

*Prerecorded weights: Before the workout the lifter and her spotter should fill in the amount of weight to be used for each exercise.

Trial and error and practical experience will be the coach's best resources for identifying start time intervals for her program. The following information will provide the coach with some guidelines for establishing start time intervals for her program.

Regardless of equipment used, the assumption is made that all athletes are performing one set of 8-12 repetitions of each exercise. Six seconds are allowed per rep (approximately 2 seconds to raise the weight and 4 seconds to lower it). The highest number of repetitions performed at any station would be 12 reps. If 12 reps are performed at 6 seconds per rep, the athlete should only spend 72 seconds actually exercising at each station.

If only one exercise is being performed at each station the coach could allow approximately 1½-2 minutes between athletes starting the program.

If two exercises are being performed at any one station—Universal gym leg curl/leg extension (Figures #5-8 & #5-9) or, Nautilus Pullover/Torso-arm (Figures #5-10 & #5-11)—the coach will have to allow more time between the starting times for the lifters.

The athletes should be encouraged to not waste time changing weights, seat settings, or moving from station to station. As the athletes become more familiar with the program, the time interval between starting times can

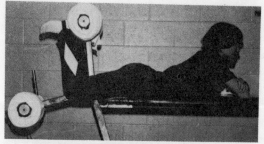

Figure 5-8. Two exercises performed at the same station.

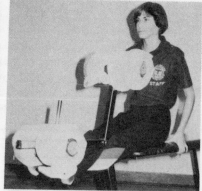

Figure 5-9.

Figure 5-10.

Two exercises performed at the same station.   Figure 5-11.

be decreased accordingly. Initially, however, the coach may have to take into consideration this "period of learning" and increase the time interval between starting times.

This method of administering a strength program will allow a coach to train a large group of athletes without sacrificing would-be-gains in muscular strength. Each athlete will be provided with the same opportunity to increase her level of strength. The coach needn't worry that some athletes may be neglecting some area of the body or overemphasizing others.

If possible, the weight room should be made available during the entire school day. If this were the case, students (with their training partner) could sign up for a start-time to work out whenever they have a free period. This would enable a larger number of athletes to make use of the program. Coaches could then encourage athletes from other teams (men and women) to make use of the program and the equipment. More participation could possibly generate interest among the school's administration to purchase additional equipment or improve the facility. If possible, faculty members, coaches, trainers, or responsible students should supervise the facility during all hours of the day to provide maximum use of the facility.

6
Barbell Workout

Individuals who are using barbells can implement the following exercises into their program. Included in the program is an exercise for each major muscle group in the body.

This program is designed to incorporate the administrative procedures outlined in Chapter 5. To implement a barbell program, the following equipment is required:

1. Eight barbells with an assortment of barbell plates at each station.
2. One power bench to perform the bench press exercise (Figure #6-1).
3. One squat rack to perform the parallel squat exercise (Figure #6-2).
4. One leg extension-leg curl station to perform those prescribed exercises (Figure #6-3).
5. Two multi-purpose benches to perform the L-seat dip exercise (Figure #6-4).
6. One chinup bar to perform the chinup exercise (Figure #6-5).
7. One set of dip bars to perform the dipping exercise (Figure #6-6).

The exercises should be performed in the prescribed order to ensure maximum efficiency.

1. Squat	8. Upright rows
2. Leg Extension	10. Good Morning
3. Leg Curl	10. Dips
4. Bench press	11. Bent-over rows
5. Chinup	12. L-seat dip
6. Side lateral raise	13. Biceps curl
7. Seated press	14. Curl-ups

Barbell Workout

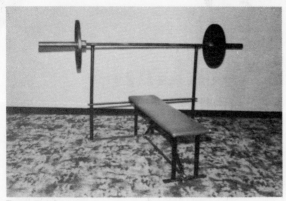

Figure 6-1.

Figure 6-2.

Figure 6-3.

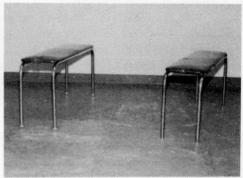

Figure 6-4.

Figure 6-5.

Figure 6-6.

One well known doctor states plainly that over 50% of sports-related injuries could be prevented through proper strength training. An increase in flexibility will generally result in a decrease in the likelihood of injury to the participant.

Figure 6-7. Do not lock the legs in the starting position.

Figure 6-8.

Figure 6-9.

EXERCISE #1: SQUAT (Figures #6-7 & #6-8)

Muscles Used: Major muscles of the legs, buttocks.

Starting Position: Standing with feet approximately shoulder width apart, barbell resting on upper back, heels elevated approximately two inches, legs are not locked out.

Description: Lower the buttocks until the middle of the thigh is parallel to the floor and recover to the starting position.

Spotting (Figure #6-9): The spotter should stand behind the lifter as close as possible to her without interfering with the lift. If the lifter needs assistance to recover to the starting position, the spotter should place her arms around the lifter's chest and pull up until the lifter is in the upright position (so that she is not bending forward at the waist) and help her raise the weight to the standing position. This technique will prevent the lifter from folding at the waist and possibly injuring her lower back.

Points to emphasize:

1. Place an adjustable stool behind the lifter and under her buttocks. The stool should be adjusted for each lifter at a height just below the position that the lifter will reach in the mid-range position. When the lifter eventually reaches the point of failure, she will be resting on the stool, thereby preventing her from falling to the floor.

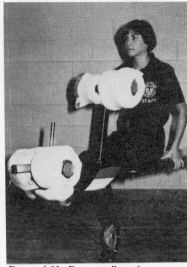

Figure 6-12.

e 6-10.

Figure 6-11. Do not allow the weight to bounce in the extended position.

EXERCISE #2: LEG EXTENSION (Figures #6-10 & #6-11)

Muscles Used: Quadriceps.

Starting Position: Sitting on the extension machine, leaning back slightly, hands grasping sides of the machine.

Description: Extend the legs forward and upward and *pause momentarily* (with no bounce) in the extended position, recover to the starting position.

Points to Emphasize:

1. Do not count a rep if the lifter cannot pause in the contracted position (Figure #6-11)
2. Keep the buttocks in contact with the pad at all times.
3. Additional padding should be placed on the rollers for comfort and more prestretching of the muscle in the starting position. (Figure #6-12)
4. This will be the only station in which two exercises are performed at the same station. The coach will have to allow an adequate time interval between athletes if both exercises are performed. Individual leg extension and leg curl stations would allow the coach to train more athletes. Suggestion: Purchase separate leg curl and leg extension stations or an additional combination leg extension-leg curl machine.

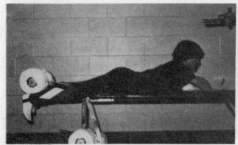

Figure 6-13.

Figure 6-14. The legs should be raised beyond perpendicular to the floor.

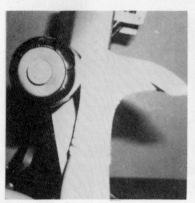

Figure 6-17.

Figure 6-15. Correct position.

Figure 6-16. Incorrect position.

EXERCISE #3: LEG CURL (Figures #6-13 & #6-14)

Muscles Used: Hamstring

Starting Position: Lying face down on the leg curl machine with the heels hooked under the pads or rollers, the kneecaps just off the edge of the pad, the toes should remain pointed toward the knees throughout the performance of the exercise (Figure #6-15 & #6-16).

Description: Flex the lower legs, raising them forward and upward as far as possible while *pausing momentarily* in the contracted position, and then recover to the starting position.

Spotting: If the lifter fails before the 12th rep, the spotter should help the lifter raise the weight to the mid-range position.

Points to Emphasize:

1. Raise the weight so that the lower legs are at least perpendicular to the floor.
2. Wrap additional padding on the rollers to provide additional stretching in the starting position (Figure #6-17).

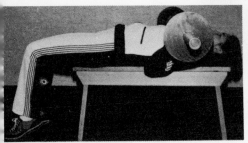

Figure 6-18.

Figure 6-19.

Figure 6-20.

Figure 6-21. The lifter is too close to the standards.

EXERCISE #4: BENCH PRESS (Figures #6-18 & #6-19)

Muscles Used: Chest, shoulders, triceps.

Starting Position: Lie face up on an exercise bench with the knees bent, the feet flat on the floor, and the barbell in the arms extended position.

Description: Lower the bar to the chest and, without bouncing the bar off the chest, recover to the starting position.

Spotting: The spotter should help the lifter raise the bar off the standards and into the starting position. If the lifter is unable to complete a repetition, the spotter should assist her only as much as is needed to complete the repetition. The lifter will eventually fail with the bar nearest the chest. Therefore, the spotter should be prepared and in a position with her hands *under* and *not over* the bar (Figure #6-20).

Points to Emphasize:

1. Do not arch the back. While this provides a mechanical advantage to the lifter, it may also injure the lifter's lower back.

2. Too often, the lifter positions herself too close to the standards of the bench. This prevents the athlete from lowering the weight in a line perpendicular to the floor because the bar, when being raised, will hit the standards causing improper technique (Figure #6-21). The lifter should position herself well away from the standards and request that the spotter get the weight out to the lifter.

Figure 6-22.

Figure 6-23.

Figure 6-24. The spotter applies
additional resistance.

Figure 6-25. Additional res
tance with a weight belt

EXERCISE #5: CHINUPS (Figures #6-22 & #6-23)

Muscles Used: Lats, biceps.

Starting Position: Pull the body upward so that the chin is over (not resting on) the bar and pause momentarily, and recover to the starting position.

Spotting: If, and when, the lifter performs negative only chins, the spotter should apply additional resistance by pulling on the lifter's hips while she lowers her body (Figure #6-24).

Points to Emphasize:

1. A weight belt is needed to add extra weight to the athlete who can properly perform 10-12 reps with her own body weight (Figure #6-25).

2. Steps are needed for the athlete who cannot properly perform at least 8-10 reps. This allows the athlete to continue performing negative-only (lowering the body in 8 seconds) chinups once she can no longer properly raise her own body weight.

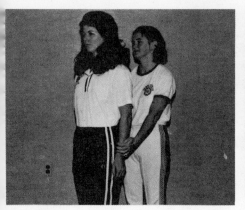

Figure 6-26.

Figure 6-27.

EXERCISE #6: SIDE LATERAL RAISE (Figures #6-26 & #6-27)

Muscles Used: Deltoids, shoulder girdle.

Starting Position: Standing with feet shoulder-width apart, arms completely extended, hands not quite touching the legs.

Description: Take two seconds to raise the arms sideward and upward to a point just above parallel to the ground, and pause momentarily. Then allow four seconds to recover to the starting position, again not allowing the hands to touch the legs.

Spotting: The spotter stands behind the lifter, with her hands on the back of the lifter's wrists. She applies some pressure in the starting position so that the lifter can't rest in that position. The spotter also applies pressure to the lifter's arms as she raises them sideward and upward, and continues to apply pressure in the mid-range position, forcing the lifter to hold that position momentarily. The spotter continues to add resistance as the lifter lowers her arms. Remember that the lifter can lower a great deal more weight, as a result the spotter should apply more pressure on the eccentric (lowering) phase of the exercise.

Points to Emphasize:

1. The spotter should force the lifter to work as hard as possible while raising and lowering the weight during each rep.
2. If the exercise has been properly performed, the lifter should find it very difficult to raise her arms (without resistance) after the last rep.
3. Keep the arms to the rear of the body, do not allow them to come forward during the execution of the exercise.

57

Figure 6-28.

Figure 6-29.

Figure 6-30. Spot under the bar.

EXERCISE #7. SEATED PRESS (Figure #6-28 and #6-29)

Muscles Used: Deltoids, pectorals, triceps.

Starting Position: Seated on an exercise bench with the barbell in the arms extended position, the feet should be hooked on the bench legs to prevent the athlete from falling backwards.

Description: Lower the weight as far as possible, not quite letting the bar touch the neck and shoulders. Without bouncing the weight off the neck or shoulders, recover to the starting position.

Spotting: Standing on the exercise bench behind the lifter, the spotter should hand the bar to the lifter and help her into the starting position Once the lifter has completed the exercise, the *spotter* should replace the bar to the floor. If the lifter fails before completing her 12th repetition, the spotter should help her raise the weight from underneath the bar (Figure #6-30).

Points to Emphasize:

1. The lifter should attempt to keep her lower back straight to eliminate any undue stress on the lower back.

2. Do not allow the arms to remain locked out. This provides the athlete with a distinct mechanical advantage and momentarily decreases the intensity of exercise. The arms can be locked out but the athlete should immediately unlock her arms and begin lowering the weight.

Figure 6-31.

Figure 6-32. Pause momentarily with the bar at the chin.

EXERCISE #8: UPRIGHT ROWS (Figures #6-31 & #6-32)

Muscles Used: Deltoids, trapezius, biceps.

Starting Position: Standing with the arms extended downward with the barbell in both hands, a closer than shoulder width grip should be used, feet shoulder width apart, head looking skyward.

Description: Pull the bar upward touching the bar under the chin and *pause* momentarily before recovery to the starting position.

Spotting: If the lifter fails before the 12th rep, the spotter should help her raise the weight; if it is too light, the spotter should apply additional resistance to force the lifter to fail by the 12th rep.

Points to Emphasize:

1. This exercise can be performed on the Universal biceps curl station or with a barbell. If the Universal biceps curl is used to perform the biceps curl, a barbell can be used at this station. This eliminates any backup that might occur if two different exercises were performed at the Universal biceps curl station.
2. Do no allow the athlete to bend forward at the waist (stand perfectly straight).
3. Allow the shoulder girdle to relax totally when the arms are completely extended.

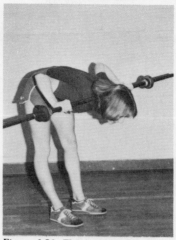

Figure 6-35.

Figure 6-33. Slightly bend forward in the starting position.

Figure 6-34. The bar should be out over the feet.

EXERCISE #9: GOOD MORNING (Figure #6-33 & #6-34)

Muscles Used: Lower back.

Starting Position: Standing, bent slightly forward, with the barbell behind the neck resting on the shoulders, feet spread shoulder width apart, legs locked, hands grasping the bar with a just wider than shoulder width grip.

Description: Bend forward at the waist and pause at a point where the upper body is below parallel to the floor, recover to the starting position.

Spotting: When the lifter fails, she will be in a position where she is bent forward at the waist and cannot recover to the upright position. The spotter should be *alert* and ready to take the bar (Figure #6-35) at that point and replace it to the floor. *Do not* perform any additional reps, once the athlete reaches that point.

Points to Emphasize:

1. *Be cautious.* Do not exercise to the point of muscular failure for the first few workouts. Gradually increase the intensity. Since most athletes ignore the lower back, a great deal of muscle soreness may be experienced. Always be cautious when exercising the lower back.

2. When lowering the weight, attempt not to move the hips backwards. Keep the weight out over the feet.

3. When recovering to the starting position, do not recover to the full upright position. This allows the lower back muscles to rest momentarily. Leave some tension on the muscles at all times.

4. Be cautious to ensure that the barbell does not roll off the back of the neck while bending forward at the waist. Pad the bar for comfort.

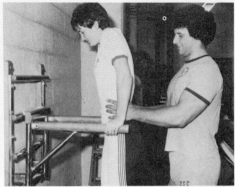

Figure 6-37.

Figure 6-36.

Figure 6-38. Extra resistance can be applied by the spotter.

Figure 6-39. A weight belt can be used for additional resistance.

Figure 6-40. Steps for negative only dips.

EXERCISE #10: DIPS (Figures #6-36 & #6-37)

Muscles Used: Chest, shoulders, triceps.

Starting Position: Mounted on the dip bars with the arms extended, legs bent (to provide full range during the lowering of the body).

Description: Bend the arms lowering the body as much as possible (Figure #6-37) and recover to the starting position.

Spotting (Figure #6-38): The spotter may have to pull on the lifter's hips to add additional resistance if the lifter is capable of performing more than 12 reps with her own body weight or during negative-only reps.

Points to Emphasize:

1. A weight belt can be used to add additional weight to the athlete who can properly perform 10-12 reps with her own body weight (Figure #6-39).

2. Negative-only dips should be performed if the athlete fails before she does 12 properly executed reps. Steps should be placed at the bottom of the dip station (Figure #6-40) to step up on and allow her to recover to the starting position.

Figure 6-41.   Figure 6-42.   Figure 6-43. Stabilize the upper
                                                                body to prevent incorrect techni◄

EXERCISE #11: BENT-OVER ROWS (Figures #6-41 & #6-42)

Muscles Used: Lats, biceps.

Starting Position: Standing with the body bent forward at the waist so that
the upper body is parallel to the floor, feet shoulder width apart,
legs can be slightly bent (to take the pressure off the lower back).

Description: Pull the barbell upward so that the barbell touches the chest,
pause momentarily, and recover to the starting position.

Spotting: N/A

Points to Emphasize:

1. A bench may be used to rest the forehead upon; this stabilizes
   the body in the bent-over position (Figure #6-43). This will also
   allow the lower back (which may still be tired from the good
   morning (exercise #9) to relax.
2. If a bench isn't used to stabilize the upper body, the athlete
   should not allow her upper body to help raise the weight. Keep
   the body stationary in a position parallel to the floor.
3. The bar should pause momentarily at the chest during each rep.
   If it does not, the spotter shouldn't count the rep.
4. Do not pull the bar toward the stomach. The bar should travel in
   a line that is perpendicular to the floor.

e 6-44.

Figure 6-45.

re 6-46.

Figure 6-47.

EXERCISE #12: L-SEAT DIPS (Figures #6-44 & #6-45)

Muscles Used: Triceps, shoulder girdle.

Starting Position: The body can be positioned between two exercise benches (Figure #6-44) or one bench can be used (Figure #6-46) making the exercise easier to perform. The hands should be shoulder width apart with the body in an "L" position.

Description: Bend the arms, lowering the body as far as possible, keeping the back against the bench as much as possible, and then recover to the starting position.

Spotting: The spotter should stand behind the lifter on an exercise bench with her hand on the lifter's shoulders. Apply as much resistance as is needed to force the lifter to fail between 8 and 12 reps. Be cautious when the lifter is in the stretched position; don't permit her to push too hard and overstretch her shoulder girdle.

Points to Emphasize:

    1. If the lifter fails before 8 reps, she can bend her legs (Figure #6-47) in order to make the exercise easier so that additional reps (no more than 12) can be performed.

Figure 6-48.   Figure 6-49.   Figure 6-50. Elbows   Figure 6-51. Incorre
                                                          remain back.   technique.

EXERCISE #13: BICEPS CURLS (Figures #6-48 & #6-49)

Muscles Used: Biceps.

Starting Position: Standing with a conventional bar or a curl bar hanging
    downward with the arms fully extended, with the upper back resting
    against a wall.

Description: Raise the bar forward and upward, contracting the biceps. The
    elbows should remain back and should be touching the wall in the
    contracted position (Figure #6-50). Pause momentarily and recover
    to the starting position.

Spotting: The spotter can manually vary the resistance during the raising and
    lowering of the weight to make the exercises more effective.

Points to Emphasize:
    1. Do not let the elbows come forward (Figure #6-51) which will
    allow the bar to become perpendicular to the floor. This will
    allow the biceps to rest momentarily unless a spotter is pulling
    back on the bar in that position. Remember that the biceps have
    contracted when the upper arm is flexed as far as possible. Mov-
    ing the elbow forward will involve the biceps but at the expense
    of letting the muscle rest in the contracted position with conven-
    tional equipment.

Figure 6-52.   Figure 6-53.

EXERCISE #14: CURL-UPS (Figures #6-52 & #6-53)

Muscles Used: Abdominals

Starting Position: Lie on back, with knees slightly bent, fingers interlaced be-. hind neck, feet flat on the floor. The upper body should be rounded to keep stress off the lower back and to a point where there is tension on the stomach muscles (Figure #6-52).

Description: Slowly curl head (tucking chin to chest) forward and continue curling upward until head and shoulders are off the floor to a point just short of being perpendicular to the floor (Figure #6-53); hold and slowly uncurl downward. Relax and repeat.

Spotting: The spotter should ensure that the lifter performs the exercise properly.

Points to Emphasize:
1. The lifter should keep her hips in contact with the floor; all bouncing or jerking movements should be strictly avoided.
2. If the lifter can execute 12 curl-ups with little difficulty, additional resistance can be added through the use of the spotter applying resistance against the lifter or from the lifter holding on to a barbell plate.
3. Take two seconds for the upward movement (1001, 1002 cadence) and four seconds for the downward movement (1001, 1002, 1003, 1004 cadence).
4. While lowering her body, the lifter should keep her back rounded to alleviate stress on her lower back. Keeping her body straight places undue stress on her lower back.

7

Universal Gym Workout

Individuals who have a Universal Gym available can implement the following exercises into their program. Included in the program is an exercise for each major muscle group in the body. This program is designed to incorporate the administrative procedures outlined in Chapter 5.

To prevent two different exercises from being performed at the same Universal Gym exercise station (Figures #7-1 & #7-2) (lat pulldown - triceps extension), the program includes several exercises that can be performed either with a barbell or on a Universal Gym.

The exercises should be performed in the prescribed order to ensure maximum efficiency;

1. Leg press
2. Leg extension
3. Leg curl
4. Bench press
5. Chinup
6. Side lateral raise
7. Seated press
8. Upright rows
9. Back extension
10. Dips
11. Lat pulldown
12. L-Seat dips
13. Biceps curls
14. Curl-ups

Figure 7-2.

Eliminate performing two different exercises at the same station whenever possible.

Figure 7-1.

Figure 7-5. Spotter assisting lifter on the first rep.

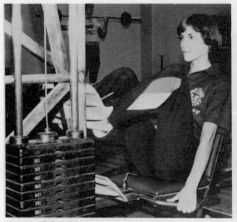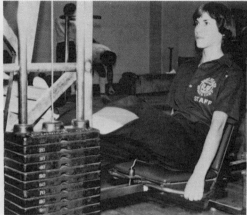

Figure *7-3 Legs just less than 90° in the starting position.

Figure 7-4. Legs not locked out.

EXERCISE #1: LEG PRESS (Figures #7-3 & #7-4)

Muscles Used: Major muscles of the legs, buttocks.

Starting Position: Seated with the middle of the foot on the leg press pedals. If upper and lower foot pedals are available, recommend that the athlete use the upper pedals. The seat should be adjusted so that the upper and lower leg form an angle of less than 90°. The hands should be placed on the side of the seat to hold the buttocks down on the seat.

Description: Extend the legs to a position just before "locking out" the legs. Do not extend the legs completely (this will allow the muscles to recover momentarily). Recover to the starting position without letting the weight plates being lifted to touch the remainder of the weight plates not being lifted.

Spotting: The spotter should place one foot on the leg pedals on the first rep to help the lifter start the exercise (Figure #7-5). If the lifter fails before performing the prescribed number of reps (12), the spotter should help the lifter raise the weight by pushing on the foot pedal with her foot. Keep in mind that the lifter will be capable of lowering the weight without assistance. If the weight is too light, the spotter can apply additional pressure to the weight stack, thereby forcing the lifter to fail by the 12th repetition.

Points to Emphasize:
1. If a headache should occur, caution the lifter to relax her shoulders and neck, then move the seat back.
2. If a separate leg extension and leg curl station is available, the leg extension exercise can be performed first and the leg press second.

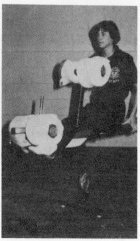

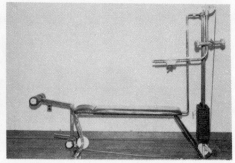

Figure 7-9.

re 7-6.

Figure 7-7.

Figure 7-8.

EXERCISE #2: LEG EXTENSION (Figures #7-6 & #7-7)

Muscles Used: Quadriceps

Starting Position: Sitting on the extension machine, leaning back slightly hands grasping sides of the machine.

Description: Extend the legs forward and upward and *pause momentarily* in the extended position, recover to the starting position.

Points to Emphasize:

1. Do not count a rep if the athlete cannot pause in the contracted position.
2. Make sure the lifter is reaching the extended position each rep.
3. Keep the buttocks on the seat at all times & don't lean forward.
4. Additional padding can be placed on the rollers for comfort and greater prestretching of the muscle (Figure #7-8).
5. This is the only station in which two exercises are performed at the same station. The coach will have to allow an adequate time interval between athletes if both exercises are performed. Separate leg extension and curl leg stations would allow the coach to train more athletes. Suggestions: Purchase separate leg curl and leg extension machines or an additional combination leg extension-leg curl station. (Figure #7-9).

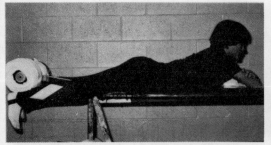

Figure 7-10.

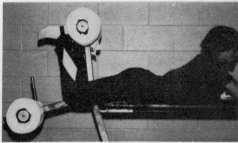

Figure 7-1

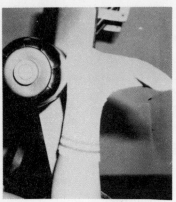

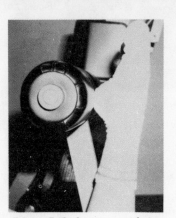

Figure 7-14.

Figure 7-12. Correct technique.   Figure 7-13. Incorrect technique.

EXERCISE #3: LEG CURL (Figures #7-10 & #7-11)

Muscles Used: Hamstrings

Starting Position: Lying face down on the leg curl machine with the heels hooked under the pads or rollers, the kneecaps should be just off the edge of the pad for maximum comfort. The toes should remain pointed toward the knees throughout the performance of the exercise. (Figures #7-12 & #7-13).

Description: Flex the lower legs raising them forward and upward as far as possible while *pausing momentarily* in the contracted position, and then recover to the starting position.

Spotting: If the lifter fails before the 12th rep, the spotter can help the lifter raise the weight to the mid range position.

Points to Emphasize:

1. Raise the weight so that the lower legs are at least perpendicular to the floor.
2. Wrap additional padding on the rollers to provide for additional stretching in the starting position (Figure #7-14).

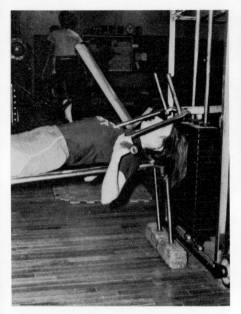

Figure 7-15. Starting position with a block of wood under the bench for greater range of movement.

Figure 7-16. Mid-range position of the bench press.

EXERCISE #4: BENCH PRESS (Figures #7-15 & #7-16)

Muscles Used: Chest, shoulders, triceps.

Starting Position: Lying on the bench with the knees bent and the feet flat on the floor. The bench press handles should bisect the middle of the chest. The bench should be elevated to place the chest muscles in a stretched position when the weight is lowered. The arms should be extended.

Description: Lower the bar to the mid-range position, and recover to the starting position. The weight plates being lifted should not touch the remainder of the weight stack in the mid-range position.

Spotting: The spotter should help the lifter raise the weight so that the lifter can begin the exercise in the arms-extended position.

Points to Emphasize:

Blocks of wood of different sizes can be used to vary the height of the bench. The thickness of the rib cage will determine how high the bench should be raised. If the bench is too low, full range exercise cannot be obtained.

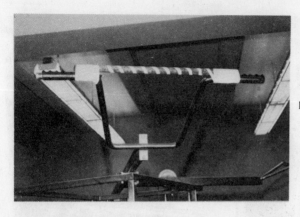

Figure 7-20.

EXERCISE #5: CHINUPS (Figure #7-17 & #7-18)

Muscles Used: Lats, biceps

Starting Position: Hanging from a chinup bar with an underhand (palms facing face) and closer than shoulder width grip.

Description: Pull the body upward so that the chin is over (not resting on) the bar and pause momentarily, recover to the starting position.

Spotting: If, and when, the lifter performs negative-only chins, the spotter should add additional resistance by pulling on the lifter's hips while the lifter is lowering her body weight (Figure 7-19).

Points to Emphasize:

1. A bar should be welded to the chin station to form one solid chin bar. This allows the athlete to take the proper width grip when performing the chinup (Figure #7-20).

2. A weight belt will be needed to add additional weight to the athlete who can properly perform 10-12 reps with her own body weight (Figure #7-21). An alternative is to have the spotter pull down on the lifter's hips to add extra resistance.

3. Steps or a ladder are needed for the athlete who cannot properly perform 10-12 reps. This allows the athlete to continue performing negative-only (the lowering phase only; takes 8 seconds for each rep) chinups once she can no longer properly raise her own body weight (Figure #7-22)

4. The attachment point of the chin bar to the machine can be used as the chinup station. Since it is closer to the floor, it precludes having the lifter climb to the much higher conventional station. It also makes negative-only chins easier and safer to perform. Pad the attachment point to prevent possible injury to the chin. The lifter should bend her legs to prevent her feet from touching the floor.

Figure 7-17.

Figure 7-18.

Figure 7-19.

Figure 7-21.

Figure 7-22.

Figure 7-23. Hands not quite touching the sides in the starting position.

Figure 7-24. Arms should be just above parallel to the floor.

EXERCISE #6: SIDE LATERAL RAISE (Figure #7-23 & #7-24)

Muscles Used: Deltoids, shoulder girdle.

Starting Position: Standing with feet shoulder-width apart, arms completely extended, hands not quite touching the legs.

Description: Take two seconds to raise the arms sideward and upward to a point just above parallel to the ground, and pause momentarily. Then allow four seconds to recover to the starting position, again not allowing the hands to touch the legs.

Spotting: The spotter stands behind the lifter, with her hands on the back of the lifter's wrists. She applies some pressure in the starting position so that the lifter can't rest in that position. The spotter also applies pressure to the lifter's arms as she raises them sideward and upward, and continues to apply pressure in the mid-range position, forcing the lifter to hold that position momentarily. The spotter continues to add resistance as the lifter lowers her arms. Remember that the lifter can lower a great deal more weight than she can raise. As a result, the spotter should apply more pressure while the lifter lowers her arms.

Points to Emphasize:
1. The spotter should force the lifter to work as hard as possible while raising and lowering the weight during each rep.
2. If the exercise has been properly performed, the lifter should find it very difficult to raise her arms (without resistance) after the last rep.
3. Keep the arms to the rear of the body, do not allow them to come forward during the execution of the exercise.

74

ıre 7-25. Feet elevated to
p the lower back flat.

Figure   7-26. Mid-range of the
seated position.

Figure 7-27.

EXERCISE #7: SEATED PRESS (Figures #7-25 & #7-26)

Muscles Used: Shoulders, chest, triceps.

Starting Position: Seated on a stool, facing away from the machine. Legs
should be bent and feet elevated off the floor (to help keep the
lower back flat). Lower back should be kept flat throughout the exercise. The higher the feet are elevated, the flatter the back will remain.

Description: Raise the weight extending the arms completely and recover to
the starting position.

Points to Emphasize:
1. Do not arch the back in an attempt to raise the weight. (Figure
#7-27). This places undue stress on the back.
2. In the arms-extended position, the bar should be directly over the
shoulders.
3. In the starting position, the handle base should be just behind the
shoulders.

Figure 7-28.   Figure 7-29.

EXERCISE #8: UPRIGHT ROWS (Figures #7-28 & #7-29)

Muscles Used: Deltoids, trapezius, biceps.

Starting Position: Standing with the arms extended downward with the barbell in both hands, a closer than shoulder width grip should be used, feet shoulder width apart, head looking skyward.

Description: Pull the bar upward touching the bar under the chin and *pause* momentarily before recovering to the starting position.

Spotting: If the lifter fails before the 12th rep the spotter can help her raise the weight; if it is too light, apply additional resistance for the remaining reps.

Points to Emphasize:

1. This exercise can be performed on either the Universal biceps curl station or with a barbell. If the Universal biceps curl is used to perform the upright row, a barbell should be used to perform the biceps curl. This will eliminate any backup that might occur if two different exercises were to be performed at the Universal biceps curl station.

2. Do not allow the athlete to bend forward at the waist (stand perfectly straight).

3. Allow the shoulder girdle to relax totally when the arms are completely extended.

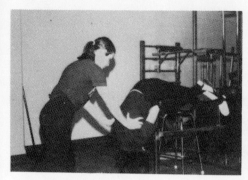

Figure 7-30. Starting position.

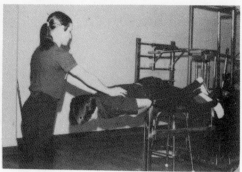

Figure 7-31. Do not raise upper body above parallel to the floor.

EXERCISE #9: BACK EXTENSION (known as a hyper extension) (Figures #7-30 & #7-31).

Muscles Used: Lower back.

Starting Position: Lying face down with the hips resting on the pad, with the upper body bent forward hanging over the bench so that the upper body is perpendicular to the floor, arms can be folded and held against the chest.

Description: Raise the body forward and upward until the body is *parallel* to the floor, *pause momentarily,* and recover to the starting position.

Spotting: The spotter should place her hands on the lifter's upper back and manually apply and vary the resistance throughout the entire exercise. The spotter must insure that the lifter does not raise her body (arch the back) above parallel to the floor.

Points to Emphasize:

1. CAUTION—While exercising the lower back, do not exercise to the point of failure during the first few workouts. Gradually increase the intensity each succeeding workout.

2. Do not arch the back! This places undue stress on the lower back, thereby increasing the chance of injury to the lower back.

3. The spotter should learn to vary the resistance while the lifter raises and lowers her body. The lifter is weaker as she raises her body and stronger during the lowering of her body. For maximum efficiency, the spotter should vary the resistance accordingly. This method of spotting is far superior to placing a weight behind the head.

Figure 7-32.   **Figure 7-33.**   **Figure 7-34.** Negative only dips can be performed by stepping up on the leg press seat.

EXERCISE #10: DIPS (Figures #7-32 & #7-33)

Muscles Used: Chest, shoulders, triceps.

Starting Position (Figure #7-32): Mounted on the dip bars with the arms extended, legs bent (to provide full range during the lowering of the body).

Description: Bend the arms, lowering the body as much as possible (Figure #7-33) and recover to the starting position.

Spotting: The spotter may have to pull on the lifter's hips to add additional resistance if the lifter is capable of performing more than 12 reps either with her own body weight or during a negative-only rep.

Points to Emphasize:

1. A weight belt can be used to add additional weight to the athlete who can properly perform 10-12 reps with her own body weight.
2. Negative-only dips should be performed if the athlete fails to do 12 properly executed reps. Steps can be placed at the bottom of the dip station or the athlete can use the back of the leg press seat (Figure #7-34) to step up on to enable her to recover to the starting position.

78

Figure 7-35.   Figure 7-36.   Figure 7-37.

EXERCISE #11: LAT PULLDOWN (Figures #7-35 & #7-36)

Muscles Used: Latissimus dorsi, biceps, posterior deltoid.

Starting Position: Assume a kneeling or seated position on the floor so that the back of the neck is directly under the bar on the lat machine. The weight plates being lifted should not be touching that part of the weight stack which is not being lifted. This will provide a prestretch in the starting position.

Description: Pull the bar downward to a position at the base of the neck and *pause* (Figure #7-36). Recover to the starting position.

Spotting: A spotter may be needed to apply pressure to the lifter's shoulders to prevent her from raising off the floor. The spotter can apply pressure to the lifter's elbows (Figure #7-37) throughout the entire exercise, allowing the lats to do more work and the biceps less. If this method is used, the lifter will need less weight.

Points to Emphasize:

1. The lat pulldown bar should be taped to provide a safer grip (chalk or resin can be available). The spotter should be alert to avoid injury to herself should the lifter's grip slip and allow the bar to dangerously move upward.

2. The lifter should lean forward slightly and *keep her body in that position.* Do not allow the lifter to lean her upper body to an upright position while recovering.

3. Do not use a wide grip. The range of movement is greater for the lats when a moderate grip is used.

79

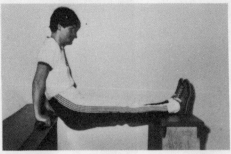

Figure 7-38.

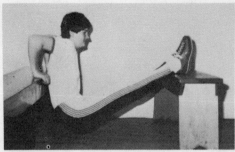

Figure 7-39.

Figure 7-40.

Figure 7-41.

EXERCISE #12: L-SEAT DIPS (Figures #7-38 & #7-39)

Muscles Used: Triceps, shoulder girdle

Starting Position: The body can be positioned between two exercise benches (Figure #7-38) or one bench can be used (Figure #7-40) making the exercise easier to perform. The hands should be shoulder width apart with the body in an "L" position.

Description: Bend the arms, lowering the body as far as possible, keeping the back against the bench as much as possible, and then recover to the starting position.

Spotting: The spotter should stand behind the lifter on the exercise bench with her hand on the lifter's shoulders. Apply as much resistance as is needed to force the lifter to fail between 8 and 12 reps.

Points to Emphasize:

1. If the lifter fails before 8 reps she can bend her legs (Figure #7-41) to make the exercise easier so that additional reps (no more than 12) can be performed.
2. The L-seat dip can be performed to place the emphasis on the triceps, as opposed to the triceps extension. This prevents two different exercises from being performed on the lat pulldown station.

Figure 7-42.

Figure 7-43.

Figure 7-44.

EXERCISE #13: BICEP CURLS (Figures #7-42 & #7-43)

Muscles Used: Biceps

Starting Position (Figure #7-42): Standing with the curl bar hanging downward with the arms fully extended.

Description: Raise the bar forward and upward, fully contracting the biceps while keeping the elbows back slightly (Figure #7-43). Pause momentarily and recover to the starting position.

Spotting: If a barbell is used the spotter should manually pull on the bar as the bar is raised and lowered to make the exercise more efficient.

Points to Emphasize:

1. Do not allow the elbows to come forward (Figure #7-44), thereby enabling the upper arms to become perpendicular to the floor. This allows the biceps to rest momentarily unless a spotter is pulling back on the bar in that position.

2. If the upright row is performed on the biceps curl station of the Universal gym, a barbell should be used to execute the biceps curl. This will prevent two different exercises from being performed on the same station.

EXERCISE #14: CURL-UPS*

*Refer to the description of how to properly perform the curl-up exercise which is presented in Chapter 6, page 65.

81

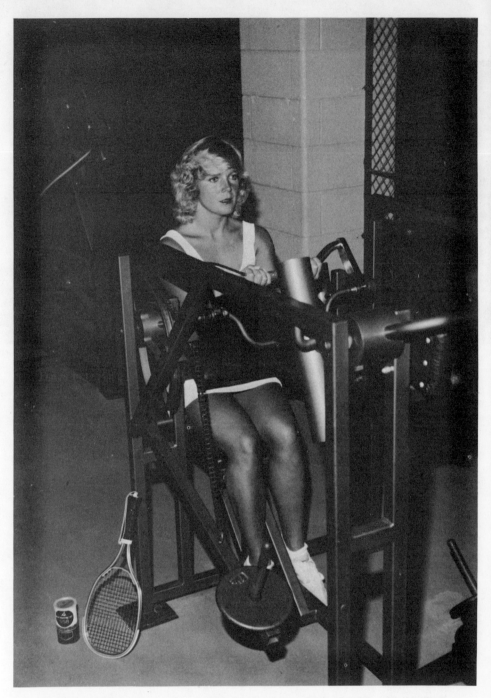

"...In fact, instructions for producing maximum results from exercise can be reduced to four words, train hard, train briefly."

Arthur Jones

8

Nautilus Workout*

Individuals who have access to Nautilus equipment can implement the following exercises into their program. The machines available will obviously determine the exercises to be performed.*

The machines discussed in this chapter include many of the basic Nautilus machines which are usually incorporated into a program. Suggestions from the manufacturer can also be your guide.

This program is designed to incorporate the administrative procedures outlined in Chapter 5. The exercises should be performed in the prescribed order to ensure maximum efficiency.

1. Hip and back
2. Leg extension
3. Leg press
4. Leg curl
5. Lateral raise
   (Double Shoulder Machine)
6. Seated press
   (Double Shoulder Machine)
7. Pullover
8. Torso arm

9. Bent arm fly
   (Double Chest Machine)
10. Decline press
    (Double Chest Machine)
11. Chinups (multi exercise)
12. Dips (multi exercise)
13. Biceps curls (curl-tricep)
14. Triceps extension (curl-tricep)
15. Curl-ups

*Nautilus Sports/Medical Industries is constantly developing additional exercise machines. Individuals who wish to obtain a current catalog of Nautilus machines should contact Nautilus Sports/Medical Industries, P.O. Box 1783, Deland, Florida 32720.

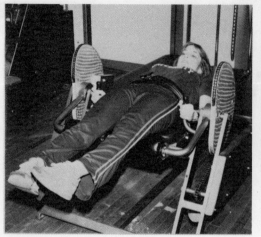

Figure 8-1.   Figure 8-2.

EXERCISE #1: HIP AND BACK (Figure #8-1 & #8-2)

Muscles Used: Buttocks, lower back.

Starting Position: Lying on the back on the Duo-Poly Hip and Back Machine
   with the ball and socket of the hip (Figure #8-3) aligned with the axis
   of rotation of the Nautilus cam (Figure #8-4), hands grasping the stationary handles, legs extended.

Description: The right leg should remain stationary in the contracted position while the left leg moves backwards to the stretched position
   (Figure #8-2) and then recovers to its starting position (Figure #8-1).
   The left leg should then remain in the contracted position while the
   right leg is moved backwards to the stretched position and then
   recovers to its starting position.

Points to Emphasize:

1. Do not pull with the hands while raising the weight (Figure #8-5).
   Keep the body in the proper starting position (Figure #8-1).
2. The leg that remains extended should not move at all while the
   other leg is being exercised.
   a. If the leg remaining in the extended position moves at any
      time while raising or lowering the weight with the other leg,
      either the weight is too heavy, the athlete is approaching
      failure, or she is coming back too far with the leg being exer-
      cised.
3. Perform 8-12 reps with each leg.

Figure 8-3. The "X" indicates the ball and socket of the hip.

Figure 8-4. The "X" on the cam indicates the axis of rotation.

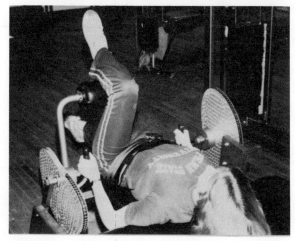

Figure 8-5.

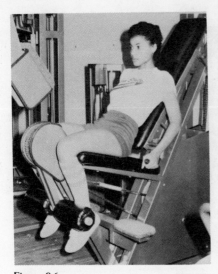

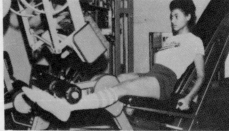

Figure 8-7.

Figure 8-6.

Figure 8-8.

EXERCISE #2: LEG EXTENSION (Figures #8-6 & #8-7)

Muscles Used: Quadriceps

Starting Position: Sitting on the Extension Machine with the feet hooked under the rollers, the back of the knee should be in contact with the front edge of the padded seat, leaning back with the hands cupped (not making a fist), grasping the hand grips available, head and shoulders back against the seat.

Description: Extend the legs forward and upward to a fully extended position and *pause momentarily;* then recover to the starting position (do not let the weight plates being lifted return to the weight stack—this allows the muscles to momentarily recover).

Points to Emphasize:

1. The same seat adjustment should be used every time the exercise is performed.
2. The lifter should reach the legs-extended position and pause momentarily for each rep. If she can't, either the weight is too ·heavy or the athlete has reached the point of failure.
3. Do not lean forward while lowering the weight; stay back in the seat.
4. Do not raise the buttocks off the seat while lowering the weight (Figure #8-8).
5. If the compound leg machine is used, the leg press exercise should be performed immediately after completing the leg extension.

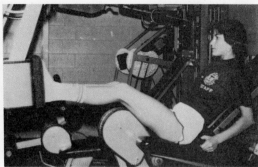

ƨure 8-9.

Figure 8-10.

EXERCISE #3: LEG PRESS (Figures #8-9 & #8-10)

Muscles Used: Buttocks, quadriceps.

Starting Position: Seated with the feet on the leg press pedals, the center of the feet placed on the middle of the leg press pedals, the seat adjusted so that the legs are being exercised through a range of movement of 90° or less.

Description: Extend the legs until they are almost extended (do not lock the legs—this allows the muscles to recover momentarily), and then return to the starting position without allowing the weight plates being lifted to touch the weight stack which is not being lifted.

Spotting: Since the exercise is started in a position where the lifter is at a distinct mechanical disadvantage, the spotter should assist the lifter to initiate the first repetition by pushing with her hands on the foot pedals of the leg press machine.

Points to Emphasize:
1. The seat should be in the same position every time the exercise is performed.
2. If headaches occur during the exercise, observe the following:
   a. Do not squeeze your hands while grasping the hand grips (cup the hands).
   b. Do not hold your breath.
   c. Move the seat back until the headache disappears.
   d. Perform the leg press first and the leg extension second.
   e. Relax the face and neck; do not shrug the shoulders.
3. The buttocks should remain in contact with the seat throughout the exercise.
4. During alternate workouts, the leg press can be performed before the leg extension and during the next workout after the leg extension.

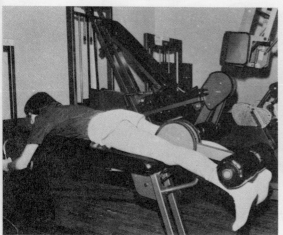

Figure 8 11.

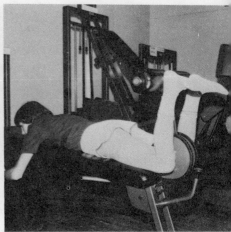

Figure 8-12. Legs must be raised at least perpendicular to the floor.

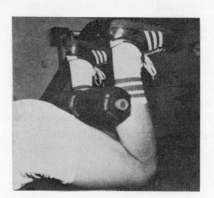

Figure 8-13A. Correct technique.

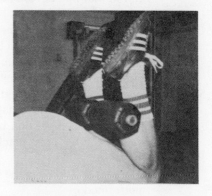

Figure 8-13B, Incorrect technique.

EXERCISE #4: LEG CURL (Figures #8-11 & # 8-12)

Muscles Used: Hamstrings.

Starting Position: Lying face down on the leg curl machine with the heels hooked under the roller pads provided, the kneecaps should be just off the edge of the pad, with the ankles flexed (toes pointed toward the knees at all times) (Figures #8-13a & #8-13b).

Description: Flex the lower legs, pulling them upward and forward until the legs are at least perpendicular to the floor, pause momentarily, and recover to the starting position, ankles should remain flexed throughout the exercise.

Figure 8-14.

Figure 8-15.

EXERCISE #5: SIDE LATERAL RAISE (Figures #8-14 & #8-15)

Muscles Used: Deltoids.

Starting Position: Seated with the ball and socket of the shoulders aligned with the axis of rotation of the Nautilus cam. Grasp the hand grips placing the back of the wrists up against the pads available, pull back on the hand grips, back resting against the seat.

Description: Raise the arms upward leading with the elbows until the upper arm makes contact with the handles used for the seated press exercise, pause momentarily and recover to the starting position.

Spotting: Once the lifter completes the side lateral exercise, the spotter should change the weight so that the lifter can immediately initate the seated press exercise.

Points to Emphasize:

1. Lead with the elbows, not the hands (Figure #8-16); do not drop the elbows, thereby pushing only with the hands.
2. If the elbows are *pulled back* and the forearms are kept *parallel* to the floor (Figure #8-17), the deltoids will be fully contracted when the elbows are just above parallel to the floor. The seat is adjusted correctly if in this position the back of the arms just barely touch the seated press handle (Figure #8-15).
3. The legs should be kept on the seat with the feet crossed.
4. Use the same seat setting each time the side lateral raise and seated press exercise is performed. The same seat setting should be used for both exercises.
5. Short individuals may need an additional pad in order to raise them to the proper seat position.

Figure 8-16. Incorrect technique—leading with hands, not the elbows.

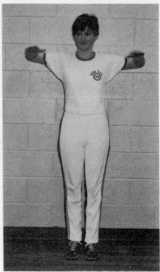

Figure 8-17. The deltoids are fully contracted in this position.

Figure 8-18.

Figure 8-19.

EXERCISE #6: SEATED PRESS (Figures #8-18 & #8-19)

Muscles Used: Deltoids, triceps.

Starting Position: Seated with the hands grasping the seated press handles, with the back resting against the pad.

Description: Extend the arms upward momentarily and recover to the starting position.

Points to Emphasize:

1. Upon completing the side lateral raise exercise, the lifter should immediately initate the seated press exercise.
2. Do not arch back.
3. Do not remain in the locked out position (Figure #8-19)

Figure 8-20.   Figure 8-21.

Figure 8-22. The X indicates the ball and socket of the shoulder is above the cam in the stretch position.

Figure 8-23. The X indicates the ball and socket of the shoulder is below the X on the nautilus cam.

EXERCISE #7: PULLOVER (Figures #8-20 & #8-21)

Muscles Used: Lats.

Starting Position: Seated with the pullover bar resting against the waist, elbows resting against the elbow pads, and the sides of the hands resting against the pullover bar (in a karate chop manner), the torso perpendicular to the floor and the seat belt secured.

Description: Lower the weight allowing the pullover bar to move upward and backward to a stretched position (Figure #8-21) and then recover to the starting position.

Points to Emphasize:

1. Do not lean forward while raising or lowering the weight.
2. Do not grab the bar, use the sides of the hands.
3. Pause momentarily with the bar resting against the stomach each rep. If the lifter cannot pause in that position, she is either using too much weight, threw the weight, or is approaching failure.
4. Adjust the seat so that the ball & socket of the shoulders (Figure #8-22), in the stretched position (Figure #8-21), is aligned with the axis of rotation of the Nautilus cam.
5. Individuals with short forearms may have to place their hands on the outside of the pullover bar (Figure #8-23).

Figure 8-24.   Figure 8-25.   Figure 8-26. Incorrect technique—The athlete is flexing the forearms which will cause forearm fatigue.

EXERCISE #8: TORSO ARM (Figures #8-24 & #8-25)

Muscles Used: Lats, biceps.

Starting Position: Seated with the arms extended and hands grasping the torso arm handles with an underhand grip. The lats should be stretched. The weight plates being lifted should not touch the weight plates which are not being lifted. The seat should be lowered from the seat setting used for the pullover exercise.

Description: Pull the bar downward, drawing the elbows back; pause momentarily, and recover to the starting position.

Points to Emphasize:

1. Do not flex the wrists while pulling the weight downward (Figure #8-26). This forces the forearm flexors to perform additional work and causes the forearms (not the lats) to reach the point of failure.
2. Do not oversqueeze the torso arm bar. Oversqueezing will also cause the forearms to fatigue.

Figure 8-27.

Figure 8-28. Pause in the contracted position.

Figure 8- 29. Incorrect technique.

Figure 8- 30. Incorrect technique.

EXERCISE #9: BENT ARM FLY (Figures #8-27 & #8-28)

Muscles Used: Pectorals

Starting Position: Seated on the Double Chest Machine with the forearms resting behind and against the arm pads on the machine (Figure #8-27). The thumbs are hooked under the top hand grips (the hand grips should meet the junction of the thumb and index finger). The elbow should be slightly higher than the ball and socket of the shoulders.

Description: Move the forearms forward leading with the elbows, until the pectorals are fully contracted, pause momentarily, and recover to the starting position.

Points to Emphasize:
1. Do not let the elbows leave the forearm pads (Figure #8-29). Lead with the elbows throughout the exercise.
2. Do not lean forward while raising (Figure #8-30) or lowering the weight.
3. Use the same seat setting each time the exercise is performed.
4. Short individuals may need to sit on an additional pad in order to raise them into the proper starting position.
5. The thumbs may have to be locked under the bottom hand grips.

Figure 8-31.

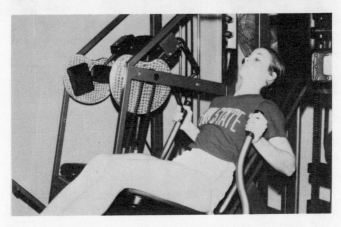

Figure 8-32.

EXERCISE #10: DECLINE PRESS (Figures #8-31 & #8-32)

Muscles Used: Pectorals, deltoids, triceps.

Starting Position: Seated (using the same seat setting that was used for the bent arm fly) on the Double Chest Machine with the decline press handles in the arms-extended position.

Descriptoin: Lower the weight while fully stretching the pectorals and recover to the starting position.

Spotting: The spotter should change the weight as soon as the lifter completes the bent arm fly so that the lifter can immediately perform the decline press.

Points to Emphasize:

    1. Do not allow the lifter to rest in the locked-out position.

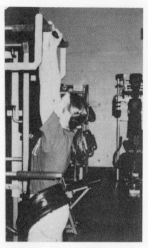

Figure 8-33.   Figure 8-34.   Figure 8-35. Incorrect technique.

EXERCISE #11: NEGATIVE ONLY CHINUPS (Figures #8-33 & 8-#34)

Muscles Used: Lats, biceps

Starting Position: Hanging from the chin bar with the arms in a flexed position, a just-closer-than-shoulder-width grip is used; the legs should be bent to prevent the feet from touching the floor; an *underhand* grip should be used; the elbows pulled back.

Description: With the weight belt attached to the hips, walk up the stairs and step off with the chin over the bar, pause momentarily in that position, and lower the body taking *eight* seconds.

Spotting: If the lifter fails before performing eight properly executed reps, the spotter should decrease the weight to permit the lifter to complete 8 reps.

Points to Emphasize:

1. Do not start the exercise with the elbows forward (Figure #8-35). Keep them pulled back (Figure #8-33).
2. The lifter should concentrate on gripping the bar only as much as is needed. Overgripping causes the forearms to fail sooner than they should.
3. When the lifter steps off the step in the starting position, she should hold that position momentarily before dropping.
4. Adjust the height of the chin bar so that when the lifter steps off her chin will be over the bar (do not let her jump to get up and over).
5. Perform only 8 reps of the negative-only chinups.

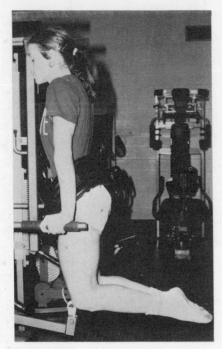 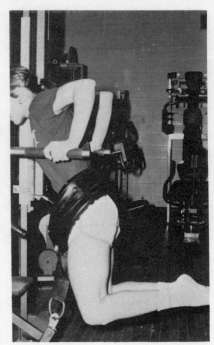

Figure 8-36.   Figure 8-37.

EXERCISE #12: DIPS (Figures #8-36 & #8-37)

Muscles Used: Chest, shoulders, triceps.

Starting Position: In the arms-extended position on the dip bars with the belt
    attached to the hips.

Description: Lower the bodyweight, taking eight seconds from the beginning
    to the end of each rep. Step off the dip bars and recover to the start-
    ing position.

Spotting: If the lifter cannot properly perform 8-10 reps, the spotter should
    decrease the weight to allow the lifter to complete the 8-10 reps
    with a lighter weight.

Points to Emphasize:

　　　1. Require the lifter to reach the fully stretched position (Figure
    #8-37) at the end of each rep.

　　　2. Do not allow the lifter to rest in the locked out position.

　　　3. As the lifter approaches the point of muscular failure, be
    cautious that she does not allow her arms to collapse from the
    extended position.

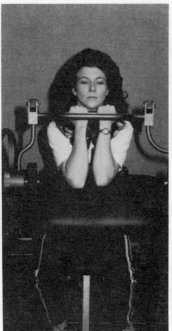
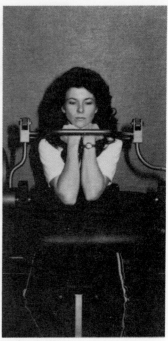

ure 8-38. An additional pad
uld be placed between the
est and the curl pad on the
chine.

Figure 8-39.

Figure 8-40. Incorrect technique.

EXERCISE #13: BICEPS CURLS (Figures #8-38 & #8-39)

Muscles Used: Biceps.

Starting Position: Seated, with a pad between the lifter's chest and the curl
pad (this keeps the lifter's torso back in the machine providing full
range exercise for the biceps). The arms should be extended and the
head and torso kept well back. Align the elbows with the axis of
rotation of the Nautilus cams.

Description: Flex the arms, raising the weight to a position where the biceps
are fully contracted; *pause* momentarily before recovering to the
starting position.

Points to Emphasize:

1. Do not touch the chin on the bar in the contracted position
(Figure #8-40). This allows the biceps to rest momentarily.
2. Do not let the elbows slide back and forth. They should remain
stationary.

Figure 8-41.

Figure 8-42.

Figure 8-43. Incorrect position.

Figure 8-44.

EXERCISE #14: TRICEPS EXTENSION (Figures #8-41 & #8-42)

Muscles Used: Triceps.

Starting Position: Seated with the side of the hands resting on the triceps extension pads in the stretched position (Figure #8-41). One or two pads may be needed to raise the athlete to a position where her arms are parallel to the floor in the extended position (Figure #8-42). If the athlete is too low in the seat her arms will not be parallel to the floor in the extended position (Figure #8-43). A wooden bar can be placed between the hands (Figure #8-44) to prevent her hands from sliding off the pads.

Description: Extend the arms completely, pausing in the contracted position before recovering to the starting position.

Spotting: The spotter should assist the lifter getting into and out of the machine by pulling the triceps extension bar over.

Points to Emphasize:

1. Use the side of the hands throughout. Do not roll the hands over, thereby placing the palms on the pads. Keep the hands in a karate chop position.

2. Do not push with the fingers and wrists in the extended position; allow the *triceps*, not the wrist flexors, to completely extend the weight.

EXERCISE #15: CURL-UPS*

*Refer to the description of how to properly perform the curl-up exercise which is presented in Chapter 6, page 65.

9

Strength Training Without Equipment

Many high school and college coaches are faced each year with the same dilemma. Their school's budget restricts their ability to expand or improve the weight training facility.

These coaches recognize the value of the many exercise devices available, yet realize that the limitations of their budget prohibit them from buying equipment they would like to have. Unfortunately, many coaches become frustrated and feel that due to a lack of equipment, a productive and organized strength program is impossible. As a result, these coaches fail to incorporate a strength training program into their programs. As a consequence, many of their athletes never obtain the benefits of a sound strength development program.

There are obvious advantages of all the different types of strength training equipment currently on the market. If funds are available, we recommend that coaches analyze the various equipment and purchase what is best for their programs.

Regardless whether or not funds are available, the coach should organize and develop a sound and productive program. With a minimum expenditure of funds, a coach can purchase and/or construct much of the equipment necessary for conducting a program.

At West Point, negative-only training has been the single most effective method of developing strength in the entering women cadets.

Coaches and athletes should remember that it is not necessarily the tool you use (that is the key to strength gains), but how you use it. A muscle needs resistance and overload for it to become stronger. If the resistance comes in the form of a sandbag, a barbell, or a machine, then so be it.

Again there are many advantages to having and using the conventional equipment which is currently available on the market. However, do not let a lack of equipment be the prohibiting factor in whether an individual participates in a properly conducted strength training program.

The program presented in this chapter is designed to develop general overall strength, using little or no equipment. Substantial gains in strength can be obtained if the lifter adheres to proper training techniques. Coaches should refer to Chapters 3 and 4 for detailed information on how to organize and administrate the program.

Many of the exercises in this program can be performed without equipment. Some of the exercises require that a few stations be constructed. The only equipment that may have to be purchased is a leg extension-leg curl machine and two barbells. A pipe inserted into two cans filled with cement can easily be substituted for the barbells if necessary.

The room required for this program does not have to be very large. A clean, well lit room with a little paint and some music can provide an attractive facility regardless of the type of equipment used. The stations should be placed in the prescribed order. Individuals should, if possible, follow the assigned order of exercises.

The following equipment is required for each exercise station:

STATION #1

A table or bench approximately six feet long, two feet wide, and three feet high can be used. The table should be padded for comfort. One end should be elevated. The table should be secured to prevent tipping. A strap will be needed to hold the lifter's legs onto the table.

STATIONS #2 and #3

A leg extension-leg curl machine to perform those specific exercises can be purchased from several models available on the market. The muscles of the legs are big and powerful. To most efficiently develop these muscles some type of exercise device is needed.

STATION #4

A barbell or something similar to a barbell is needed. No more than 150 pounds will be needed. An adjustable stool is also needed.

STATIONS #5 and #6

A chin bar and dip bar is required with steps provided to recover to the starting position. Ideally 2 chin bars and 2 dip bars are needed.

STATION #7

Two pads are needed to elevate the hands to perform the pushup exercise. This will provide the proper stretching of the chest and shoulders and allow for full range exercise. During the conventional pushup, since the chest touches the floor, the chest muscles are not fully stretched.

STATION #8

No equipment is necessary. The spotter should manually provide the resistance. The same area can be used to perform Exercise #7 and #8. A mirror can be strategically placed on the wall to help the lifter and spotter properly perform the exercise.

STATIONS #9 and #10

If a Penn State chinup-dip station is constructed, there will be two chinup and two dip stations available. Therefore, the same station will be the unit used for exercises 5 and 6, and 9 and 10.

Authors's Note: Remember that chinups and dips are two of the most productive exercises that can be performed. They involve both the pushing (dips) and the pulling (chins) muscles of the body.

STATION #11

A barbell weighing approximately 30-50 pounds will be needed.

STATION #12

Two benches or chairs can be used to elevate the feet and hands to perform the "L" seat dip exercise.

STATION #13

An abdominal board can be constructed or a pad on the floor can serve the same purpose.

MANUAL RESISTANCE EXERCISES:

A spotter can manually provide resistance to a lifter in the same manner that a barbell or machine does. Remember that the muscle does not know who or what is providing the resistance. This method of resistance training can be just as productive as any mode of resistance if the spotter and lifter properly coordinate the exercise.

On all manual resistance type exercises, the spotter should learn to properly vary the resistance to accommodate the lifter's change in strength as the lifter raises and lowers the resistance. Several guidelines which both the lifter and spotter should follow are:

1. The lifter and spotter should communicate whenever necessary to provide for a more efficient exercise.
2. Once the lifter begins performing an exercise, she should not relax or rest between repetitions. The spotter should learn to keep the tension on the muscles from the beginning of the exercise to the end.

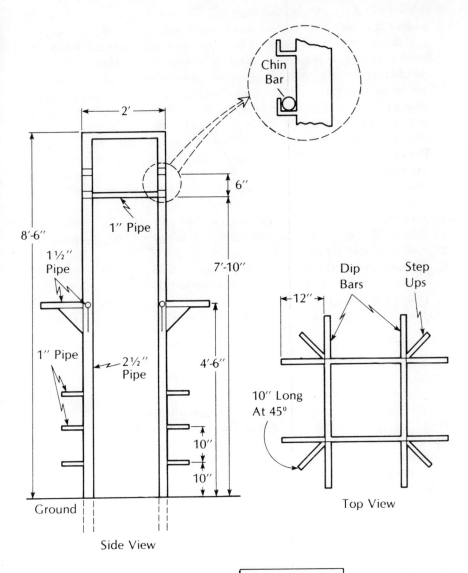

Chin Bar

2'

6"

1" Pipe

8'-6"

1½" Pipe

7'-10"

1" Pipe

2½" Pipe

4'-6"

10" Long At 45°

Dip Bars

Step Ups

12"

10"

10"

Ground

Side View

Top View

Chin-Dip Station

Drawn by Bill Crummy Penn State
Class of '79

3. While raising the weight, the lifter will be stronger at some points and weaker at others. The spotter must recognize this and develop a feel for applying more resistance where the lifter is stronger and less where the lifter is weaker. If the spotter properly applies the resistance, the lifter should feel a steady, controlled, smooth amount of resistance while raising the weight. If the spotter applies too much resistance at any point, the lifter's movement will either be stopped or she will be forced to either jerk or use other improper techniques to raise the weight.

4. The lifter can lower a great deal more weight than she can raise. Therefore, the spotter should manually apply more resistance during the lowering action of the exercise. The transition from the (amount of resistance applied) raising to the lowering of the weight should be a smooth one.

5. If the exercise is properly performed, the lifter will gradually grow weaker each succeeding repetition. The spotter should, therefore, decrease the resistance accordingly.

6. The spotter should force the lifter to work as hard as possible during the execution of each of the 10-12 repetitions performed for each exercise. (Perform at least 10 repetitions but no more than 12 repetitions).

The following exercises should be performed in the prescribed order:

Exercise	Major Muscles Developed
Back extension	Lower back
Leg extension	Quadriceps
Leg curl	Hamstrings
Squat	Major muscles of the legs
Dips	Chest, Shoulders, Triceps
Chinups	Upper back, Biceps
Pushups	Chest, Shoulders, Triceps
Side lateral raise	Shoulders
Chinups	Upper back, Biceps
Dips	Chest, Shoulders, Triceps
Biceps curls	Biceps
L seat dips	Triceps
Curl-ups	Abdominals

EXERCISE #1: BACK EXTENSION*

*Refer to the description of how to properly perform the back extension exercise which is presented in Chapter 7, page 77.

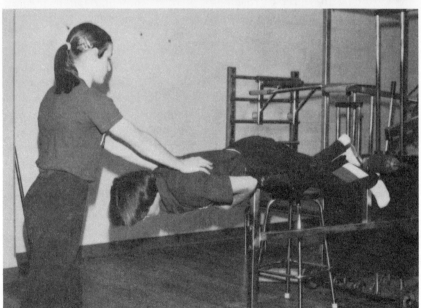

To avoid undue stress on her back, a lifter should not arch her back while performing the back extension exercise.

EXERCISE #2: LEG EXTENSION*

*Refer to the description of how to properly perform the leg extension exercise which is presented in Chapter 6, page 53.

EXERCISE #3: LEG CURL*

*Refer to the description of how to properly perform the leg curl exercise which is presented in Chapter 6, page 54.

EXERCISE #4: SQUAT

Starting Position: Standing with a bar across the shoulders with the legs slightly bent and the heels slightly elevated (approximately 2-3 inches); legs slightly bent.

Description: Lower the buttocks to a position where the middle of the thigh is just below parallel to the floor, pause momentarily (without bouncing), and recover to the starting position.

Spotting: The spotter will place her hands on the lifter's shoulders or pull on her hips and apply additional resistance each repetition forcing the lifter to reach the point of muscular failure (cannot stand up) somewhere between 10 and 12 repetitions.

Points to Emphasize:
1. While performing the squat it is recommended that the lifter allow four seconds to *raise* the weight and *four* seconds to lower the weight. By allowing four seconds to raise the weight it will reduce the need for a heavy barbell and provide a safer form of exercise. A 125 pound barbell should provide more than enough resistance if the spotter properly spots the exercise.
2. Use an adjustable stool and adjust the height of the stool to suit each athlete. When the athlete reaches the point where she can no longer stand up (somewhere between 10 and 12 repetitions), she should safely rest on the stool and allow the spotter to replace the bar to the floor (Figure #9-1).
3. Do not allow the lifter to lock her legs when she stands up. This allows her to rest and momentarily recover.

Figure 9-1.   Figure 9-2.   Figure 9-3.

EXERCISE 5: DIPS (Figures #9-2 & #9-3)

Starting Position: Mounted on the dip bars with the arms extended and the legs flexed.

Description: Bend the arms and lower the body to a fully stretch position; then recover to the starting position.

Spotting: The spotter's responsibility is to force the lifter to reach the point of muscular failure somewhere between 8 and 12 repetitions. If the lifter can properly perform more than 12 repetitions with her own body weight, the spotter should manually pull on the lifter's hips adding extra resistance causing the lifter to eventually fail between the prescribed number of repetitions.

Points to Emphasize:

   1. If the lifter is unable to perform and complete 12 repetitions with her own body weight, she can make up the difference with negative-only dips. She can recover to the starting position using the steps provided on the Penn State chin-dip station and just lower the body weight taking *eight seconds.* The spotter should continue to apply additional resistance while the lifter lowers her body.

Figure 9-4.

Figure 9-5.

Figure 9-6.

EXERCISE 6: CHINUPS (Figures #9-4 & #9-5)

Starting Position: Hanging from the chin bar with the arms fully extended. An underhand grip (palms facing the face) should be used.

Description: Pull the body upward until the chin is resting over the bar, pause momentarily, and recover to the starting position.

Spotting: If the lifter can perform more than 12 repetitions with her body weight, the spotter can apply additional resistance by pulling on the lifter's hips causing her to fail on or before the 12th repetition.

Points to Emphasize:
1. If the lifter is unable to perform and complete 12 repetitions with her own bodyweight, she can make up the difference with negative-only chinups. She can recover to the starting position using the steps provided on the Penn State chin-dip station (Figure #9-6) and then lower her body weight taking 8 seconds. The spotter should continue to apply additional resistance (as much as the lifter needs) to force an all out effort by the lifter.

EXERCISE 7: PUSHUPS (Figures #9-7 & #9-8)

Starting Position: Elevate the hands (with pads) from two to four inches off the floor and assume the pushup position.

Description: Lower the chest to a position where it is fully stretched but not touching the floor. Pause momentarily and recover to the starting position.

Figure 9-7.

Figure 9-8.

Figure 9-9.

Figure 9-10.

Spotting: The spotter should straddle the lifter and place her hands on the lifter's upper back (Figure #9-7). The spotter should apply as much resistance to the lifter's upper back as needed to stimulate an all out effort. If the spotter properly spots the exercise, the lifter should not be capable of recovering to the starting position with only her body weight on the last repetition.

Points to Emphasize:

1. Do not allow the lifter to arch her back (Figure #9-8). This could .place undue stress on the lower back.

2. If the lifter reaches the point of failure (cannot extend her arms) before performing 10-12 repetitions, she should drop to her knees (Figure #9-9) and continue performing the exercise (in modified, positive fashion).

3. If the lifter is unable to raise her body after dropping to her knees the spotter may have to help pull her up to the starting position (Figure #9-10) so that the lifter can complete 10-12 repetitions of the exercise.

4. Once the lifter is unable to perform the exercise in the (positive) modified fashion, she can perform additional repetitions in a negative-only fashion (refer to Chapter 3).

EXERCISE 8: SIDE LATERAL RAISE*

*Refer to the description of how to properly perform the side lateral raise which is presented in Chapter 7, page 74.

EXERCISE #9: CHINUPS

Starting Position: Refer to Exercise #6
Description: Refer to Exercise #6
Spotting: Refer to Exercise #6
Points to Emphasize:
1. The chinup exercise is performed again to substitute for another pulling movement (lat pulldown, bent over row, seated row). The same muscles are used to perform any pulling movement.
2. An overhand grip can be used for variety.

EXERCISE #10: DIPS

Starting Position: Refer to Exercise #5
Description: Refer to Exercise #5
Spotting: Refer to Exercise #5
Points to Emphasize:
1. The dip exercise is performed again to substitute for another pushing movement. The same muscles are used to perform any pushing movement.

EXERCISE #11: BICEPS CURL*

*Refer to the description of how to properly perform the biceps curl which is presented in Chapter 6, page 64.

EXERCISE #12: L-SEAT DIPS*

*Refer to the description of how to properly perform the l-seat dips which is presented in Chapter 6, page 63.

EXERCISE #13: CURL-UPS*

*Refer to the description of how to properly perform the curl-ups which is presented in Chapter 6, page 65.

10

Flexibility Program

Flexibility is one of the basic elements composing an individual's level of fitness. For every athlete, in particular, it is very important that she strive to achieve (and increase where necessary) an adequate level of flexibility in each of the major muscle groups of the body.

An increase in flexibility can decrease the incidence or minimize the severity of some injuries. An increase in flexibility can improve performance. For example, a longer length of stride can result in an increase in speed of movement. Or an increase in flexibility might allow a field hockey player to get lower in her game stances, thereby improving her game skills. However, the prevention of injury is the *primary* advantage of a flexibility program.

We recommend that all athletes engage in an organized (supervised by the coaches) session of stretching before each game or practice. A brief jog around the field before stretching may help increase circulation and facilitate the warming up process.

Coaches should supervise each stretching exercise of every stretching session. Unfortunately, athletes will typically place little emphasis on stretching if the coach is not interested enough to supervise the program.

Different philosophies exist in the area of stretching. We suggest that all stretching movements be controlled without any bouncing or jerky movements. Bouncing (dynamic) movements could hyperstretch some muscle fibers causing fiber tears. This may cause some unnecessary soreness and possible scar tissue to develop.

The most accepted mode of stretching at the present is a method called passive stretching. While stretching, the athletes should place a mild stretch on the muscle and hold the stretch without forcing the muscle to be over-stretched. Bob and Jean Anderson's book, titled *Stretching,* is one of the best available references on flexibility.

Stretching can and should be done daily. To maintain and continue to increase flexibility, an athlete must stretch daily during the preseason, during the season, and during the off season.

Enclosed is the program that should take approximately 7 minutes to complete. We recognize that some coaches recommend that more time be spent during the pre-game (pre-practice) stretch. Every coach and athlete must decide for themselves what portion of the available time should be allotted to conditioning and what portion to the practice of skills. Obviously, the less time that she spends in the area of conditioning, the more time she has to improve her skills. We believe that the following program can meet the needs of most programs. To save time on the field, the coach should use the following checklist to conduct the stretching program. The coach should teach her athletes how to perform each exercise and assign each exercise with a name.

To administer the program the coach should stand among her athletes with a whistle and use a stopwatch to control the amount of time spent on stretching. If the enclosed program is used, the coach should sound off with the name of the exercise, allow the athletes to assume the stretched position and hold it for the prescribed amount of time indicated on the checklist. When the allotted time is up for the stretching exercise, the coach should blow the whistle and announce the next exercise. This procedure should be used until each of the exercises has been performed.

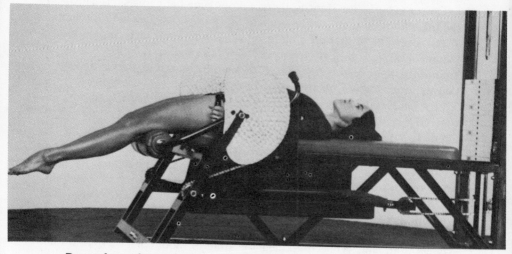

Properly performed exercise will increase—not decrease—flexibility.

Pre-Game or Pre-Practice Stretch Checklist

(For the coach or athlete to use before a game or practice)

1. Stretch the Neck
   "Pull it forward" - 5 seconds - whistle
   "Push it back" - 5 seconds - whistle
   "Pull it left" - 5 seconds - whistle
   "Pull it right" - 5 seconds - whistle
   "Look left" - 5 seconds - whistle
   "Look right" - 5 seconds - whistle
2. "Scratch the back with the right arm and lean left" - 10 seconds - whistle
3. "Scratch the back with the left arm and lean right" - 10 seconds - whistle
4. "Handcuff" - 10 seconds - whistle
5. "Touch the toes" - 15 seconds - whistle
6. "Cannonball" - 10 seconds - whistle
7. "Grab the ankles" - 10 seconds - whistle
8. "Grab the toes" - 10 seconds - whistle
9. "Grab the instep" - 10 seconds - whistle
10. "Butterfly" 20 seconds - whistle
11. "Spinal twist right" - 10 seconds - whistle
12. "Spinal twist left" - 10 seconds - whistle
13. "Right foot to the armpit" - 10 seconds - whistle
14. "Left foot to the armpit" - 10 seconds - whistle
15. "Right sole to the thigh" - 10 seconds - whistle
16. "Left sole to the thigh" - 10 seconds - whistle
17. "Butterfly" - 10 seconds - whistle
18. "Cannonball" - 5 seconds - whistle
19. "Legs over" - 15 seconds - whistle
20. "Sit up and reach out down the middle" - 10 seconds - whistle
21. "Reach right" - 10 seconds - whistle
22. "Reach left" - 10 seconds - whistle
23. "Quad stretch right leg" - 10 seconds - whistle
24. "Roll it over" - 15 seconds - whistle
25. "Quad stretch left leg" - 10 seconds - whistle
26. "Roll it over" - 15 seconds - whistle
27. "On your mark, right leg back" - 10 seconds - whistle
28. "On your mark, left leg back" - 10 seconds - whistle

"Begin Practice"

Figure 10-1. Pull it forward.

Figure 10-4. Pull it right.

Figure 10-2. Pull it back.

Figure 10-3. Pull it left.

EXERCISE #1 - STRETCH THE NECK

Muscles Stretched: Neck Muscles

Starting Position: Standing with the neck muscles totally relaxed head looking downward, hands interlocked behind the head (Figure 10-1)

Description: Step 1 - pull forward with the hands placing a mild stretch on the back of the neck and hold for 5 seconds (Figure 10-1)

Step 2 - Look skyward, pulling the head backwards with the hands (Figure 10-2) placing a mild stretch on the front of the neck and hold for 5 seconds.

Step 3 - Look straight ahead and pull the head to the left (with the left hand - Figure 10-3), placing a mild stretch on the right side of the neck and hold for 5 seconds.

Step 4 - Pull the head to the right (with the right hand - Figure 10-4), placing a mild stretch on the left side of the neck and hold for 5 seconds.

Step 5 - Look to the right as far as possible and hold for 5 seconds. (Figure 10-5).

Step 6 - Look to the left as far as possible and hold for 5 seconds. (Figure 10-6).

114

EXERCISE #2 - SCRATCH THE BACK (Figures 10-7 & 10-8)

(with right arm and lean to the left)
Muscle Stretched: Shoulder girdle, side of rib cage.
Description: Standing with the right arm bent and the right hand reaching down the center of the back as far as possible. The left hand will pull on the right elbow placing a mild stretch on the shoulder girdle (Figure 10-7). The athlete will slowly lean to her left and hold that position for 10 seconds (Figure 10-8)

EXERCISE #3 - SCRATCH THE BACK

(with the left arm and lean to the right)
Description: Mirror exercise #2

EXERCISE #4 - HANDCUFF (Figure 10-9)

Muscles Stretched: Chest, shoulder girdle
Description: With the arms extended the athlete should interlock her hands behind the back. She should slowly push the chest forward and pull the arms toward each other placing a mild stretch on the chest and shoulders (hold for 10 sec.).

EXERCISE #5 - TOE TOUCH (Figure 10-10)

Muscles Stretched: Hamstrings, back, calves.
Starting position: Legs straight, body bent forward at the waist, totally relaxed.
Description: Step 1 Slowly bend forward placing a mild stretch on the back and legs and hold for 10 seconds.
Step 2 - Relax and repeat step 1, trying to increase the range of movement during step 2 (hold for 15 seconds).
Points to Emphasize:
1. Do not try to touch the toes immediately if the athlete does not already possess that range of movement. Gradually increase the stretch during the exercise.
2. No bouncing
3. The goal of all athletes should be to place the palms on the floor and hold it (Figure 10-11).

EXERCISE #6 - CANNONBALL (Figures 10-12 & 10-13)

Muscles Stretched: Lower and upper back
Starting Position: (Figure 10-12) Seated with knees pulled up to the chest and the arms wrapped around the legs.
Description: Roll backwards keeping the chin tucked and the body in a tight ball (Figure 10-13). Continue a rocking motion back and forth for 10 seconds.

EXERCISE #7 - ANKLES - TOES - INSTEP (Figures 10-14, 10-15, & 10-16)

Muscles Stretched: Lower and upper back, hamstrings, calves.

Starting Position: Seated with the legs straight.

Description: Step 1 - Reach forward grabbing the ankles (Figure 10-14) and hold for 10 seconds and relax.

Step 2 - Reach forward and grab the toes (Figure 10-15) and hold for 10 seconds and relax.

Step 3 - Reach forward and grab the instep of the feet (Figure 10-16) and hold for 10 seconds.

Points to Emphasize:

1. Keep the legs locked throughout the exercise.

EXERCISE #8 - BUTTERFLY (Figure 10-17)

Muscles Stretched: Groin, lower and upper back.

Starting Position: Seated with the legs bent and the soles of the feet together. Pull the heels toward the groin. The arms should be outside and over the legs.

Description: Pull the upper body forward and apply pressure to the legs, pushing them downward. Place a mild stretch on the groin and hold for 20 seconds.

Points to Emphasize:

1. The goal of the athlete should be to reach a point where she can flatten both legs to the ground and simultaneously touch the forehead to the feet.

EXERCISE #9 - SPINAL TWIST (Figure 10-18)

Muscles Stretched: Lower and upper back, hips

Step 1 - Spinal Twist Right (Figure 10-18)

Starting Position: Seated with the right leg bent and crossed over the extended left leg. The right hand should be placed on the ground directly behind the athlete. The left arm (elbow) will be placed against the right leg. The head should be looking to the right as far as possible.

Description: The player should pull with the left arm (on the right leg) and look to the right placing a mild stretch on the lower and upper back for 10 seconds.

Step 2 - Spinal twist left (Figure 10-19)

Description: Mirror step (Left leg over right & look to the left).

EXERCISE #10 - FOOT TO THE ARMPIT (Figure 10-20)

Muscles Stretched: Hips

Step 1 - Right foot to the left armpit.

Starting Position: Seated with the right leg bent and the left leg extended. The right arm is wrapped around the right leg and the left hand is holding the right foot.

Description: With the left hand, pull the right foot toward the left armpit simultaneously pulling the right knee (with the right arm) toward the body. Hold for 10 seconds.

Step 2 - Left foot to the right armpit (Figure 10-21)

Description: Mirror step 1 (pull the left foot toward the right armpit.

EXERCISE #11 - SOLE TO THE THIGH

Step 1 - Right sole to the thigh (Figure 10-22).

Muscles Stretched: Back, hamstrings, groin.

Starting Position: Seated with the right leg bent and the sole of the right foot placed against the inside of the left leg. The upper body should be bent forward and the hands reaching for the left leg.

Description: Bend forward pulling with the hands, placing a mild stretch on the back and hamstrings and hold the stretch for 10 seconds.

Step 2 - Left sole to the thigh (Figure 10-23)

Description: Mirror step 1

EXERCISE #12 - BUTTERFLY

Starting Position: Same as Exercise #8.

Description: Same as Exercise #8.

EXERCISE #13 - CANNONBALL (Figures 10-12 & 10-13)

Starting Position: Same as Exercise #12

Description: Same as Exercise #12-13

EXERCISE #14 - LEGS OVER (Figure 10-24)

Muscles Stretched: Lower back, hamstrings.

Starting Position: Lying on the upper back and shoulders with the legs straight and the body bent at the waist.

Description: The athlete should pull the toes toward the ground keeping the legs straight and hold for 15 seconds.

Points to Emphasize:

1. The athlete may begin the exercise with legs slightly bent and gradually straighten the legs and work the toes toward the ground.

EXERCISE #15 - SIT UP & REACH OUT

Muscles Stretched: Lower and upper back, hamstrings, groin.

Starting Position: Seated with the legs spread apart.

Step 1 - Down the middle (Figure 10-25).

Figure 10-5. Look right.

Figure 10-6. Look left.

Figure 10-7. Scratch the back.

Figure 10-8. Lean left.

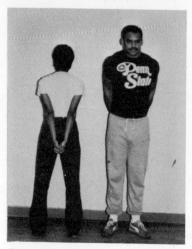

Figure 10-9. Handcuff.

Figure 10-10. Toe touch.

Figure 10-11. Palms on the ground.

Figure 10-12. Cannonball.

Figure 10-13. Cannonball.

Figure 10-14. Grab the ankles.

Figure 10-15. Grab the toes.

Figure 10-16. Grab the instep.

Figure 10-17. Butterfly.

Figure 10-18. Spinal twist right.

Figure 10-19. Spinal twist left.

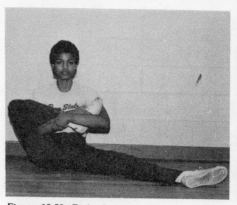

Figure 10-20. Right foot to armpit.

Figure 10-21. Left foot to armpit.

Figure 10-22. Right sole to thigh.

Figure 10-23. Left sole to thigh.

Figure 10-24. Legs over.

jure 10-25. Reach out
wn the middle.

Figure 10-26. Reach right.

jure 10-27. Reach left.

Figure 10-28. Quad stretch
with the right leg.

Figure 10-29. Roll it over.

Figure 10-30.

Figure 10-31.Quad stretch with the left leg.

Figure 10-32. On your mark with the right leg back.

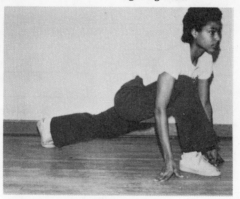

Figure 10-33. On your mark with the left leg back.

Description: Bending forward at the waist, the athlete should reach out as far as possible placing a stretch on the back and legs and hold for 10 seconds.

Step 2 - Reach right (Figure 10-26)

Description: Bending sideward (to the right) and forward, the athlete should attempt to touch her nose to her right knee.

Step 3 - Reach left (Figure 10-27)

Description: Bending sideward (to the left) and forward the athlete should attempt to touch her nose with her left knee.

EXERCISE #16 - QUAD STRETCH

Quad Stretch with the Right Leg (Figures 10-28 & 10-29)

Step 1 - Starting Position: Lying on the left side with the right hand grabbing the right foot (Figure 10-28)

Description: The athlete should pull on the foot placing a stretch on the right quadricep and hold it for 10 seconds.

Step 2 - Roll it over (Figure 10-29)

Starting Position: Seated with the left leg straight and the right leg bent with the right toe tucked under the buttocks (Figure 10-29).

Description: The athlete should gradually move the upper body backwards placing a stretch on the right quadriceps and eventually reach the fully stretched position (Figure 10-30) and hold for 15 seconds.

Points to Emphasize:

1. Initially most athletes will not be able to assume the fully stretched position. Do not overstretch. Gradually increase the range of movement each succeeding workout.

Quad Stretch with the left leg. (Figure 31)

Step 3 - Mirror Step 1. (Figure 10-31)

Step 4 - Mirror Step 2.

EXERCISE #17 - ON YOUR MARK (Figure 10-32)

Muscles Stretched: Groin, guadricep, hamstring.

Step 1 - With the right leg back (Figure 10-32)

Starting Position (Figure 10-32): The legs are split with the left leg forward and the right leg back. The left foot should be flat on the ground and the right knee behind it.

Description: The body would be moved forward placing a stretch on the groin and leg and held for 10 seconds.

Step 2 - With the left leg back (Figure 10-33)

Starting Position: Mirror step 1.

Description: Mirror Step 1.

REFERENCES:
Anderson, Bob; *Stretching,* P.O. Box 2734, Fullerton, California, 92633

Any athlete who hopes to maintain her pre-season level of strength must maintain her strength *DURING* the season.

11

In-Season
Strength Training

While strength training has increasingly been accepted as a means of improving performance and preventing injury, there are some aspects of a sound strength training philosophy which have met with resistance. For example, while most coaches recognize the value of strength training and have made it an integral part of their overall conditioning program—*during the off-season,* relatively few teams employ an *in-season* strength training program.

Unfortunately, the emphasis on an in-season strength training program is usually either minimal or totally non-existent. We believe this is a mistake. Athletes should develop additional strength during the off-season and at least attempt to maintain their strength during the season. It is counterproductive for an athlete to ignore the need for and the benefits of an in-season strength training program. Since athletic performance depends to a great extent upon physical parameters involving explosive power, speed of movement, and short term muscle endurance, any athlete who hopes to maintain her pre-season strength level must maintain her strength *during* the season.

Where the athlete fails to take action to maintain her strength level during the season, a significant decrease in the physical attributes that depend primarily upon strength will result. The decrease in strength will also leave the athlete more susceptible to injury as the season progresses.

In-Season Strength Training

Chart 1

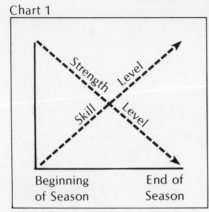

Chart 2

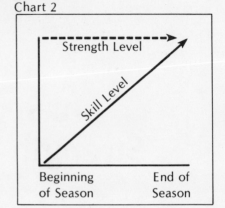

Chart 1 shows that as the season progresses, the athlete's skill level (timing, jumping, throwing, catching, running) will improve. If, however, she doesn't adhere to a strength maintenance program, her strength level will decrease as the season progresses.

The athlete's *peak performance potential* (where her strength level and skill level bisect on the chart) will probably occur somewhere during the middle of the season. Unless her strength is maintained, the athlete will probably never achieve her full performance potential.

Practicing the sport itself (contrary to popular belief) does not enable an athlete to maintain her level of muscular strength. Any muscle that isn't properly overloaded at least every 72 to 96 hours will begin to grow gradually weaker and smaller. For example, if during the athlete's last workout before the season begins, she lifts 100 pounds for ten reps. To maintain that strength level during the season (or for as long as she wants) the athlete must lift 100 pounds for ten reps every 72 to 96 hours. In short, the coach should be cognizant of the fact that the athlete's strength level will begin to drop approximately 72 to 96 hours after her last workout in the weight room, and will continue to decrease until she engages in another strength workout.

Ideally, the athlete should peak near the end of the season when her skill level approaches its peak. As can be observed in Chart 2, this can (and should) be accomplished by a strength maintenance program conducted throughout the season. The athlete can maintain and continue to gain strength to some extent with two workouts per week.

For maximum efficiency the first workout should be performed the day after the game and the second workout between 48 to 72 hours before the next game. Working out the day after the game helps alleviate stiffness and soreness and enables the athlete to recover fully for a brief mid-week workout. During the workout the day after the game, the athlete should engage in a general total body workout similar to a workout she would perform during the off-season.

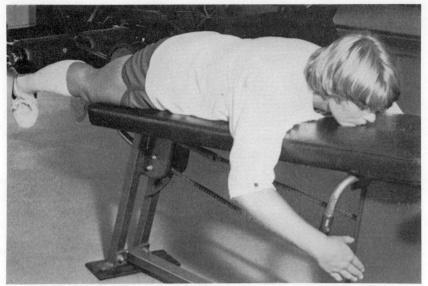

Conditioning should be a year-around commitment.

The program should be administered using those principles discussed in Chapter 5. Athletes should be paired off and assigned a start time. The day-after-workout can be performed using (in the prescribed order):

1. Leg press	5. Side lateral raise	9. Dips
2. Leg curl	6. Seated press	10. Bent-over rows
3. Bench press	7. Upright rows	11. L-seat dip
4. Chinups	8. Good morning·	12. Biceps curl

It should be noted that only one exercise is being performed at each exercise station. This allows the coach to assign start times approximately every 72 seconds apart. As soon as the athlete finishes the first exercise (leg press), she immediately proceeds to the next exercise (leg curl) while another athlete immediately begins training at the vacant leg press station.

If the coach allows 80 seconds between training teams, she could train at least 46 players in approximately 1½ hours.

Due to limitations on time and facilities, it's usually difficult, if not impossible, to train the entire team during the mid-week workout. One possible alternative is to split the team and work half the squad out on alternate mid-week days. Another possibility is to train the entire team on upper body exercises one day and on lower body exercises another day. The same amount of time could be realized if the entire squad worked out two consecutive days—half the team performed the upper body exercises on Day #1 and the lower body exercises on Day #2. The other half of the team members would reverse the training schedule.

Adherence to a scientifically-based strength training program will produce results where they count...in the athletic arena.